RSPB BOOK OF
Garden Birds

RSPB BOOK OF
Garden Birds

by Linda Bennett

with 36 plates in colour by
C. F. Tunnicliffe R.A.

and line drawings by
Robert Gillmor

Hamlyn
London · New York · Sydney · Toronto

To my parents

The painting of House Martins on page 97 is reproduced
by kind permission of Trevor Gunton

Published by The Hamlyn Publishing Group Limited
London · New York · Sydney · Toronto
Astronaut House, Feltham, Middlesex, England

Reprinted 1979, 1980

ISBN 0 600 31422 7

Phototypeset by Tradespools Limited, Frome, Somerset
Colour separations by Culver Graphics, Slough, England
Printed in Great Britain by Loxley Brothers Limited, Sheffield

Contents

What is a garden bird?

Since gardens are unnatural habitats created by man, the category garden birds is also artificial. Gardens themselves are extremely variable, from a tiny backyard in the centre of a city to a large, mature country estate. In this book I have tried to choose the most common and interesting birds that are found in gardens but, inevitably, many people may never be visited by all the species listed, whereas others may be able to add to my selection.

Over the ages man has shaped the landscape to suit his needs. He has felled woods, created moorland, drained marshes and ploughed downland so that the British landscape is now a compromise between man and nature. Surprisingly, we do not appear to have lost many woodland species and the overall number has not been seriously affected because the majority of woodland birds are found around the edges and in the forest glades. Thus, as man broke up the large forests making hedgerows and parkland, he provided even more suitable habitats for these species. Later, the development of villages and towns with their gardens created an entirely new habitat which was also ideal for the woodland-edge birds.

Censuses of all the species breeding in a suburban area have shown that the birds are at the same density as in mixed woodland (12.5 birds per hectare [5 per acre]), are slightly more plentiful than in pure deciduous woods and over twice as dense as on grassland. Some species, such as the Blackbird, find gardens far better to live in than their traditional woodland habitat. In gardens, they are found at a density of about 8 to 10 pairs per hectare (3 to 4 per acre), whereas in woodland, there is less than one pair for every 2 hectares (5 acres); therefore, they

are more than twenty times as plentiful in gardens.

It thus comes as little surprise that the majority of garden birds are woodland-edge species. However, some are better adapted to garden life than others. Blackbirds and Song Thrushes nesting in gardens produce over four times the number of successful nests as in woodland, and twice as many as on farmland. Dunnocks do one-and-a-half times as well in gardens and on farmland as in woods, whereas Chaffinches fledge young from twice as many suburban as woodland nests but have their highest success rate when nesting on farmland.

Life is not all roses in the garden for all woodland species; for example, Great and Blue Tits are not so well adapted to nesting in the garden as in their original woodland habitat. They both lay smaller clutches in gardens and at least eight times as many chicks die due to starvation. What is more, those that fledge are smaller and therefore stand less chance of surviving the autumn and winter.

The crucial difference between the tits and the thrushes is that the former are true woodland birds relying on the rich insect food found in oak communities to feed their young. Blackbirds and Song Thrushes, however, are woodland-edge birds which thrive in the mixed habitat of the garden with shrubs, flowerbeds and lawns.

Other species have found it less easy to adapt to garden nesting but, they do move in when food is short. Marsh and Willow Tits, woodpeckers and some of the winter visitors such as the Redwings, Fieldfares and Waxwings are good examples; as more people put out food the bird list increases. Siskins have suddenly discovered peanuts which they prefer in red mesh bags; and a few Blackcaps, instead of migrating, now winter in Britain relying on bird-tables for their food. In a hard winter, feeding birds in the garden can have a significant effect on the population. In the winter of 1962–63 at least a million birds' lives may have been saved by food on bird-tables.

However, not all garden birds are of woodland origin. The Starling and House Sparrow have always been closely associated with man, feeding on his leftovers and waste, and nesting in his houses. Their whole ecology is now completely geared to our own. Collared Doves could not have colonized Britain's cities so successfully were it not for urban gardens, which provide secure nesting and roosting places within commuting distances of the docks and grain mills.

The aerial insectivores, the Swifts, Swallows and House Martins also rely heavily on man; they have now almost completely abandoned their natural nest-sites in trees and on cliffs in favour of his buildings. They hunt over the man-made habitats of gardens and farmland, and recent control of air pollution has allowed them to move into city centres.

Marshland and waterbirds, which were most affected by man's changes to the landscape, have been slow to make use of gardens. However, Pied Wagtails can now be seen chasing insects across a lawn and Reed Buntings are beginning to feed on bird-tables in winter. A pond or stream in the garden will allow Moorhens and possibly a Kingfisher to join the garden bird category.

The abundance of birds in our gardens has inevitably attracted some predatory birds. All members of the crow family are fond of smaller birds' eggs and nestlings; the Jackdaw, Magpie and occasionally the Jay have moved into the garden where there are rich and easy pickings. Occasionally Sparrowhawks or Kestrels will catch birds feeding on the bird-table, but the main bird predator in the garden is the Tawny Owl. This nocturnal hunter has even moved into town and city centres to feed on the plentiful supply of Starlings and House Sparrows.

The importance of this rich garden bird community becomes especially apparent in Cambridgeshire, where I live. Here, much of the land is made up of vast, prairie-like fields without a tree or hedge in sight. The villages with their gardens, not only relieve the monotony, but provide vital oases for all forms of wildlife.

It would be unrealistic to say that man should not have destroyed the natural environment of Britain by building towns where woods once grew or draining the Cambridgeshire fens to create farmland. As population increased so did the need for somewhere to live and to grow food, and thus areas for wildlife inevitably diminished. It may seem that there is very little a single individual can do, but there is no need to be a defeatist. You can help in two ways: by supporting the voluntary wildlife conservation organizations so that they can acquire and manage areas as reserves for wildlife, and by improving your garden to provide a bird reserve of your own.

Gardens and their birds through the ages

It is unlikely that Bronze or Iron Age man was a gardener in the true sense of the word. However, he did change the natural landscape by felling and clearing the forests for cultivation and grazing, which doubtless produced suitable habitats for many of the birds that we now associate with farmland.

The Romans were the first people in Britain to lay out gardens as we know them today. Although we have no description of English Roman gardens, no doubt they were similar to those elsewhere in Europe. These consisted of lawns with geometrical designs formed by low, clipped hedges of box, privet or laurel – not the ingredients of a bird paradise. However, the outer areas of paddocks planted with fruit trees, walks of ivy-covered trees, pergolas supporting vines and creepers and fountains sound much more promising. Furthermore, the Romans often favoured wilder areas containing clumps of native shrubs and trees which are just what one advises for modern bird gardens.

Very little is known of the birds in this period, except from the bones found in Roman settlements, which reflect a diet of ducks, geese and game rather than the total avifauna. Of the birds mentioned in this book only the Barn Owl, Jackdaw, Jay, Song Thrush and Dunnock have been found. The first four were presumably eaten or kept as pets but perhaps the Dunnock was found scurrying around beneath those clipped, box hedges. A small bronze of a Robin from the end of the Romano-British period suggests that it, too, was a familiar garden bird.

Little is known of gardens in the Dark Ages, except for those in the monasteries where vegetables and herbs were grown and extensive orchards and vineyards were maintained; the nobles probably retained gardens like the Romans. It is during this period that the written record of our garden birds begins, with the story of a Robin kept as a pet by St Serf of Culross in Fife, in AD 530. By the end of the eighth century a further twenty garden birds had been added to the list. Many of the references occur in riddles. These identify the birds so clearly that the monks and poets who wrote them must have been most observant bird-watchers. They knew something of their habits too; for instance the Goldfinch was called the 'thistle tweaker'.

By the time of the Norman conquest, over half the birds mentioned in this book had been recorded. For the next 400 years gardens were designed to provide food, herbs and medicines. Fittingly, one of the few records of garden birds in this period was of an invasion of Crossbills attacking cider apples in the West Country.

The sixteenth and seventeenth century saw the development of elaborate symmetry in the garden; flowerbeds in the shape of knots surrounded by neatly clipped box, privet and thorn hedges. By the end of the sixteenth century over 80 per cent of our garden birds had been recorded and the first bird book, William Turner's *Avium Praecipuarum*, had been published. Soon after, an act was passed to protect grain and other produce; this listed the pest species and the bounties awarded for destroying them. Bullfinches were classed as vermin for the damage they caused to fruit buds in orchards, and the price on their heads was one penny.

The seventeenth century produced the first real field ornithologists – John Ray and Francis

Willoughby who travelled throughout the country studying birds. They distinguished many difficult species such as Coal from Marsh Tit and Chiffchaff from Wood Warbler (but not yet from Willow Warbler). By 1700, 95 per cent of the garden birds had been identified.

In the eighteenth century there was a great change in garden design from the formal arrangements of beds and hedges to a more natural structure, with many shrubs and trees on different levels and elaborate lakes and water-works typical of the gardens of Capability Brown. These gardens offered much more to birds and there was an indication that people were beginning to appreciate the beauty and value of nature.

It was during this period that the enclosure of common land took place which transformed our countryside into the pattern we see today. It also deprived the working man of his common rights and he was therefore given a piece of ground around his house or an allotment where he could grow his own food; this was a cheaper alternative for the landlord than paying out higher wages. From this stems the traditional feeling among the English that a house should have a garden. This tradition has resulted in the development of an urban and suburban environment that is suitable for birds and wildlife but is an extravagant use of land.

With garden designs returning to nature and every man feeling he had a right to a garden, it was at the beginning of the nineteenth century that the first bird gardeners appeared. John Dovaston was unlike his contemporaries, who managed their estates for shooting, as he would not allow birds to be killed or molested on his land. It is thought he was the first person to invent a feeding device for wild birds. He describes this 'Ornithotrophe' in a letter to Thomas Bewick, the famous wood-engraver, in 1825. It consisted of a wooden trencher suspended from three harpsichord wires on a ring and was designed to move along a cord outside his study window. He fixed perches around it and fastened half-picked bones and pieces of mutton to the trees. On a snowy winter's day he recorded twenty-three species at his trencher. He also tried to provide natural food by growing mistletoe berries for the birds. He caught Robins visiting his feeders and marked them by clipping parts of their plumage, and this led him to discover that each bird possessed a territory. He published his findings nearly ninety years before Eliot Howard, who is generally credited with this discovery, produced the classic book, *Territory and Bird Life*.

In 1843, Charles Waterton, another conservationist ahead of his time, declared his estate in Yorkshire a bird sanctuary. He was probably the first person in Britain to create artificial nest-sites for wild birds. He built ingenious bird houses for Starlings, drilled holes or made doors in decaying stumps and converted a hollow oak into a two-storey house for owls with a built-in observation seat in the lower half. He planted holly 'fortresses' for roosting birds and encouraged ivy to grow over several ruined buildings to provide nest-sites.

Through the examples and writings of these two men, the idea of feeding birds and providing nesting places for them spread. In 1877, a letter appeared in *The Times* to encourage people to feed the birds. However, it was not until the hard winter of 1890–91, when all the leading newspapers ran a campaign to promote the feeding of birds, that the practice became widespread.

Meanwhile in Germany in the 1880s, Baron von Berlepsch was perfecting the housing and feeding of birds on his estate. Not only did he delight in the birds themselves but reasoned that they would help to control insect pests in his forests. The park and woods around his castle were carefully laid out and shrubs and trees pruned to encourage birds. He hung up numerous nest-boxes of various sizes and designs for different species. All were made out of sections of natural tree trunks, and apart from the conventional hole nest-box, he also perfected an open-fronted box for flycatchers and a horizontal Swift box.

His artificial feeding was based on three methods: first, a food-tree with branches onto which he poured melted suet containing a mixture of bread, dried meat, seeds, berries and ants eggs, providing food for both insectivorous and seed-eating birds; secondly, a food-house which was an elaborate roofed structure like a bird-table with two-tiered feeding trays; and thirdly, a food-bell that was an automatic dispenser of birdseed. It is a sobering thought that things have changed little in bird gardening in the last 100 years.

Back in England, the Fur and Feather group was founded in 1889 to protest against the use of bird feathers for millinery. Two years later it became the Society for the Protection of Birds and widened its objectives to all aspects of bird protection. In 1904, the Society gained its Royal charter and two years later moved into the field of bird gardening. In volume two of the RSPB's publication, *Bird Notes and News* (the precursor of *Birds*) an advertisement appears offering for sale a variety of nest-boxes for one-and-sixpence or two shillings each.

Gardening for birds

To make your garden attractive for birds it is quite unnecessary to start from scratch with a mechanical bulldozer and spend a fortune on shrubs and trees at the local garden centre. With a little thought, whether your garden is new or established, you can help improve the habitat for wildlife.

If your garden is spotlessly tidy and you are constantly raking, pruning, mowing and spraying against every pest, it will remain birdless. To attract birds the garden must contain the essentials of their natural environment. Therefore, it should not be too neat and should contain plants (preferably native) that provide food, nesting places and shelter. However, do not assume it must look like a wilderness covered with hawthorns and thistles. It is perfectly possible to strike a happy medium between exotic and native shrubs, or neat tidy borders and patches of weeds and brambles.

Planning the garden

Whether you are starting from the bare soil left by the building contractors or simply remodelling your established garden, it is best to map out a basic plan. On a piece of graph paper draw the outlines of your garden sheds, garage, existing paths and fences. Note the soil type, existing trees, the sloping areas and shaded ones and any other physical characteristics that may be important when choosing your new shrubs. With your plan completed there are a few points to bear in mind for successful bird gardening.

You, and not the birds, should dictate the final result. However, choose plants that provide useful food and shelter and which will offer an attractive environment for birds as well as yourself.

Wind direction is important. Most human beings hate cold winds and so do birds, and so it is commonsense to shelter your garden on the north and east sides with a good thick hedge.

Levels are also important; do not think of your garden as a two-dimensional area. If you go into a wood you will notice that there are four main levels: the ground, the herbs and tall grasses, the shrubs and the trees. Choose plants for your garden that will give a wide range of heights. However, remember to consider the eventual size of trees and shrubs in relation to your garden; an all too frequent mistake is the selection of varieties that eventually become far too large for the allotted site.

Straight lines are almost non-existent in nature, so forget about your ruler when making the plan. A square lawn bordered by neat, rectangular beds is both unnatural and monotonous. A few curves and irregular edges will make the birds feel far more at home. Also, natural areas are seldom flat; a small, south-facing rockery or bank adds variety and is less likely to become completely snowed over in hard weather.

Plants are seasonal, therefore, check on the times when they flower and produce berries. Try to select a combination of plants that provide food and shelter throughout the year.

When planting new trees try to choose native species. These are better suited to our climate, are part of our natural pattern of flora and fauna and support a variety of insects which are both interesting in their own right and provide food for birds. However, do not assume you can remove your new trees from the local woods.

It is illegal to dig up any plant without permission from the landowner, whether it is an oak sapling, a dog rose or a primrose; but you can take cuttings or collect seeds. It is far better to purchase strong, healthy specimens from a good nursery as they will have a much better chance of survival.

The importance of water

Birds need water throughout the year for both drinking and bathing. It can be as great an attraction as food especially in built-up areas where water may be in short supply during dry weather. Have you noticed the way different species drink? Swallows and Swifts take a passing sip on the wing; Doves and Pigeons take a long draught; and most garden birds fill their beaks and tip their heads back, letting the water run down their throats.

The joy of a bath for your garden birds is not to have a good long soak. This would make their feathers brittle and damage the water-proofing properties. Before preening they need to damp their feather lightly as this helps to spread the oil from their preen gland which is situated at the base of the tail. Regular preening is essential to keep a bird's plumage in tip-top condition.

Unless you are lucky enough to have a stream or pond in the garden already, you will have to provide water by some sort of artificial means. Birdbaths are the most obvious way. They can be purchased from garden centres but are often expensive, aesthetically displeasing and badly designed so that they do not fulfil their primary purpose. There are two types of ideal bird-baths. Both are made of fibreglass and one can be placed directly on the ground whereas the other is raised on a pedestal.

Basically, any shallow container will make an adequate birdbath providing the birds can reach the water without slipping. A simple bath can be made from an upturned dustbin lid either sunk into the ground or supported on three bricks. A few rocks in the bottom will make it easier for the birds to reach the water. In winter, freezing is a problem but thermostatically controlled heaters, such as those used in aquaria, can be placed in the bottom of the pool and covered with gravel. However, do make sure the wires are adequately insulated for outdoor use. Alternatively, if your bath is raised up on bricks and is heat-proof, a slow-burning night-light covered with a flowerpot can be placed beneath it.

If you have plenty of room in your garden a small pond is the ideal solution. You can then grow an attractive variety of water plants and also keep a few goldfish. Newts, frogs, dragon-flies and other insects will soon be attracted to the pond and you may even be honoured by the presence of the more unusual garden visitors such as a Kingfisher or a Heron.

Making a suitable pond is quite easy. First, decide on its position. It is best sited where you can watch it from a window but it should not be too close to any bushes which could conceal a cat or any other predator. A slight bank on the north side of the pond is desirable, for this will catch the sun and be sufficient to thaw the ice at the edge on cold mornings.

Decide on the shape and size of your pond and mark it out with string. The hole needs to be about 120cm by 150cm (4ft by 5ft); the deepest part should be at least 60cm (2ft) and the bottom should slope gradually to a shallow end. When you have dug your shape remove as many of the sharp stones as possible from the sides and bottom. Line the hole with several layers of newspaper – wet them if it is a windy day to prevent them blowing away. The newspaper will protect the polythene lining from being punctured by stones or broken roots. Now you are ready for the heavy duty polythene layer, which should be at least 1 000 gauge and about 300cm by 250cm (10ft by 8ft) in area. Lay the sheet carefully in the hole allowing a large overlap all round and trap the edges with flat stones or with the turf you have removed. Spread a layer of soil, about 5 to 8cm (2 to 3in) thick over the sheet and place a couple of rocks near the edge so that they will stick out of the water. Fill your hole with water and allow the pond to settle for a week before planting.

The aquatic plants can be grown in the soil layer at the bottom of the pond. However, you are less likely to damage the polythene lining if rooting plants are grown in old buckets or special wire baskets. Plants are vital to keep your pond healthy and fresh. Yellow flag (*Iris pseudacorus*), amphibious bistort (*Polygonum amphibium*), meadowsweet (*Filipendula ulmaria*), branched bur-reed (*Sparganium erectum*) and club-rush (*Scirpus lacustris*) will grow round the edge, while some good plants for the deeper area include waterlilies (*Nymphaea alba* or *Nuphar lutea*), hornwort (*Ceratophyllum demersum*), Canadian pondweed (*Elodea canadensis*) and starwort (*Callitriche* spp.). Frogbit (*Hydrocharis morsus-ranae*) and water soldier (*Stratiotes aloides*) are suitable free-floating plants.

Collect some pond snails and water beetles (make sure both carnivorous and herbivorous species are included) from a nearby pond as they will help to create a natural community.

After digging out to the required shape and depth remove all sharp stones

Line the hole with newspaper and then lay polythene sheeting to overlap all round

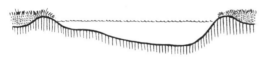

A shallow end will allow birds to bathe

Secure the edge of the polythene before filling

Water is important for birds and a garden pond will provide drinking and bathing facilities.

Maintenance of a well-balanced pond will be minimal but, if it is situated under trees remember to clear away the fallen leaves in the autumn. The growth of algae is natural and harmless, but in hot weather this may proliferate and need cleaning out. In hard weather the ice must be broken every day so that the birds can drink.

Dust-bathing

Some birds, such as sparrows and Wrens, also like to dust-bathe in order to keep their feathers in good condition and remove parasites. A shallow box or pit filled with a mixture of equal parts of sand, soil and sieved ash makes an ideal dust-bath which is best positioned in a sheltered, sunny spot, facing south. When you have first built the dust-bath it is a good idea to bait the area with a handful of seeds.

Worming grounds

A lawn, even a very small one, is important in a bird garden. Although grass itself is not a bird food the seeds are taken by Dunnocks, finches and sparrows. Also, a lawn full of worms, insect larvae and pupae is an excellent hunting ground for Blackbirds, thrushes and Robins. Secluded lawns may even be visited by Green Woodpeckers in search of ants.

Although worms castes can sometimes look unsightly, never treat your lawn to kill the worms. Apart from providing a good meal for birds (and even foxes) their burrowing helps soil drainage and aerates the grass roots. If you simply brush the lawn, the fine, rich soil from the castes will improve the growth of the grass.

On hot, dry summer days a finely-set lawn spray will not only water the grass but will also attract birds which like to bathe and catch worms that may come to the surface. In autumn, do not be too hasty in clearing away your leaves as they also encourage the worms.

Trees and shrubs for birds

Carefully chosen trees and shrubs can provide the three basic requirements for birds – food, shelter and nest-sites. Very often all three go together; if you grow plants for food they can usually be pruned to provide nesting-sites and shelter.

The number of potential nesting places in your garden can be greatly increased by judicious trimming. A closely clipped privet hedge less than 1m (3ft) high is no good at all for nesting birds as it is too thick and low. Similarly, a closely pruned japonica may produce beautiful blossom but will have few branches suitable for supporting a nest.

In general, hedges or trees should be cut in such a way that they grow into forks. If four or more branches sprout from the same point an ideal site can be created by cutting out the central stem. Young shrubs can be pruned each year to produce a series of forks at different levels. Each plant will present its own problems and possibilities and therefore it is a question of trial and error. The angle of the fork is important; it should be about 70° and pointing directly upwards. However, if it is facing slightly sideways nesting will still be possible. The fork should be made of not less than three branches and preferably more. You can only prune trees or shrubs to provide these natural nest-sites if their branches grow at suitable angles. Those of spruce are too wide, cypress is too narrow and the branches of weeping trees fall in totally the wrong direction.

Hedges should be trimmed so that they are about 2m (6ft) high and at least 60cm (2ft) thick. It may also be necessary to thin out the hedge so that there is room for the birds to fly in and out. Climbing shrubs, such as cotoneaster, pyracantha and honeysuckle need to be cut back fairly severely to produce thick growth from several points; the clusters of foliage will make excellent nesting places for flycatchers and Blackbirds. Pergolas and ornamental archways offer good sites for finches and thrushes and an old apple tree is ideal for Goldfinches.

If your garden is to be used the whole year round, places where the birds can shelter and roost are just as important as nest-sites. A thick stand of bushes or trees provides the best protection against wind, rain or snow. It is particularly important in the winter months when birds spend as many as sixteen hours at their roosts. Evergreen foliage, such as holly, rhododendron and laurel, offers the best sites. However, when beech is grown as a hedge it retains its leaves throughout the winter so it is almost as good. A hedge of this sort is best planted on the north or east side of the garden to keep off driving wind and rain. A discarded Christmas tree also offers shelter and will bear seeds when mature. Ivy-covered trees are popular roosting sites as the birds can change their position according to the prevailing wind. A well-grown bramble patch is another very popular roosting site with sparrows and finches.

If you want to see a variety of birds in your garden it is also important to provide natural foods. Trees and shrubs for food fall into two categories; those that attract insects and those that bear fruit and berries.

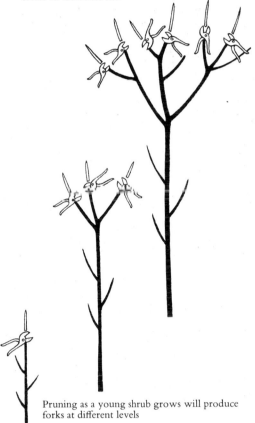

Removal of the central stem from a shrub will create an ideal nest-site

Pruning as a young shrub grows will produce forks at different levels

You can increase the number of nest-sites offered by trees and shrubs by careful pruning.

Undoubtedly the most productive of our native trees is the oak. It supports so much insect and other wildlife that it is almost a habitat in itself. However, oaks take a long time to mature and need a lot of space, and therefore you may prefer to plant a quicker-growing species. Silver birches attract numerous small insects on which all types of tits feed. Many insects, especially moths, lay their eggs on willow leaves and their grubs are eaten by Robins, tits, Wrens and Dunnocks. Poplars provide excellent elevated song-posts for thrushes and also support a number of caterpillars. Ordinary fruit trees, such as apple and pear, have good rough bark which houses many insects and grubs. A dead, rotting stump will harbour a wealth of insect life for tits, Nuthatches, Treecreepers and woodpeckers; it may also have a hole or two for nesting. Let it decay in peace and if you feel it is unsightly a climbing plant such as clematis or honeysuckle can be grown up against it.

Berry-bearing shrubs are a valuable source of food for thrushes, Starlings, finches, tits, Robins and pigeons and, you may even attract some Waxwings, Redwings or Fieldfares – winter visitors from Scandinavia. However, do remember that although several plants produce berries that are eaten by birds, they are poisonous to man and domestic animals.

A list of useful trees and shrubs for birds could fill half this book. However, the following list includes the berry-bearing shrubs which have been shown to be popular food for birds. A few species that offer good nesting or roosting sites are also mentioned. It is worth bearing in mind that native species support more insect life than non-native, and are therefore even more attractive to birds.

Barberry *Berberis darwinii*
2–3m (6½–10ft); all soils; non-native

If barberry is well clipped it forms a good, thick, prickly hedge which will provide safe nest-sites for thrushes, finches and Dunnocks once it reaches 1.5–2m (5–6½ft) in height. Its berries are eaten by at least nine species of birds in the autumn.

Blackberry or bramble *Rubus fruticosus*
up to 2m (6½ft); calcareous to neutral clays and loams; native

If you have room for a bramble patch in one corner of your garden it will be used by birds throughout the year. Blackbirds, thrushes, warblers, finches, Long-tailed Tits and Dunnocks will all nest in the safety of its prickly

fastness. In the RSPB's survey of berries as bird foods, seventeen species fed on blackberries; it was a particular favourite of Blackbirds, Bullfinches, Starlings, Great Tits and Blue Tits. In autumn and winter finches and sparrows will gather in your bramble patch to roost as they do in my own. To prevent the plant invading the garden trim the long tendrils each year and stop them rooting; this will also keep the patch thick and attractive to birds.

Cotoneaster *Cotoneaster horizontalis, C. simonsii, C. watereri*
1–3m (3–10ft); most soils; non-native

All species of cotoneaster produce excellent berries for birds and can provide food from August until March. The fruits are commonly eaten by Blackbirds and thrushes, Bullfinches, Greenfinches and House Sparrows. However, a well-berried cotoneaster could provide the highlight of your garden birdwatching year – a view of a Waxwing – as the berries are great favourites of this extremely tame winter visitor. Cotoneasters are not very good for nesting but a well-pruned, mature specimen against a wall might house a Blackbird or thrush.

Crab apple *Malus* spp.
M. sylvestris native
3–10m (10–32½ft); well drained loams

There are a great variety of cultivated crab apples all of which produce fruit eaten by birds. In the RSPB survey seven different species including the thrushes, Woodpigeons and Waxwings fed on crab apples and the most popular species was *M. pumila*. A mature tree might also be used by a nesting Chaffinch or Goldfinch.

Elder *Sambucus nigra*
up to 10m (32½ft); chalky to neutral loams; native

Many people think of elder as a weed, nevertheless its dark purple berries were top favourites in the RSPB survey. Thirty-two species fed on elder and it was particularly sought after by thrushes and Starlings. Elders grow very rapidly but if the new growth is trimmed back by about 30cm (1ft) each year it will provide nest-sites for Blackbirds, thrushes, Chaffinches and Bullfinches. The hollow trunk of an old tree is a favourite breeding place for tits and sparrows.

Firethorns *Pyracantha* spp.
3–5m (10–16ft) all soils; non-native

Firethorns are very good shrubs to train against the house where thrushes and even a Spotted

Barberry

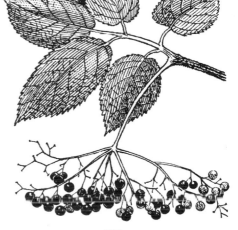

Crab apple

Blackberry

Elder

Cotoneaster

Firethorn

Flycatcher will nest. The orange berries are taken by at least eleven species of birds including Mistle Thrushes, Redwings and Waxwings.

Flowering currant *Ribes sanguineum*
1–2m (3–6½ft); well drained loams; non-native

Flowering currant berries are normally eaten by thrushes, but those of the red and blackcurrant are occasionally taken by Blackcap, Whitethroat and Garden Warbler.

Hawthorn *Crataegus monogyna*
2–10m (6½–32½ft); most soils; native

Blackbirds, Redwings, Fieldfares and Waxwings were among the twenty-two species that were recorded gorging themselves on the dark red haws of hawthorn in early winter. This shrub provides excellent nesting-sites for thrushes, finches, buntings, warblers, Woodpigeons and Magpies as it keeps out both cats and small boys. When grown as a hedge, be careful not to trim back the new shoots to exactly the same height every year or the hedge will become too thick and woody for nesting; leave about 15cm (6in) of new growth. Hawthorn can be left to grow free as an attractive standard tree.

Holly *Ilex aquifolium*
up to 15m (49ft); well drained soils; native

Holly trees are of much greater value for birds if grown as a clump rather than a thick, trimmed hedge which is impenetrable. Blackbirds, thrushes and Greenfinches will nest in the younger bushes and Mistle Thrushes, Collared Doves and Woodpigeons in larger trees. Since it is evergreen, holly provides protection from the weather all the year round and makes excellent roosts. The berries are taken by a number of birds but are especially favoured by Redwings, Starlings and Woodpigeons. Hollies have separate male and female plants so if you want berries plant mainly females.

Honeysuckle *Lonicera* spp.
L. periclymenum native
up to 6m (19½ft); all soils

Honeysuckle is a delightful climber to have in the garden. It will clamber over a hedge, old tree stump or archway, brightening the spot with its beautiful flowers and strong scent, and will attract a feast of insects for birds. Prune it hard and it will produce thick, bushy growth to provide ideal nesting and roosting cover. Its berries are also a popular food. Japanese Honey-

suckle *L. japonica* is an evergreen and therefore provides good cover all the year round.

Ivy *Hedera helix*
up to 30m (97½ft); any soil; native

Ivy is often accused of strangling trees; however, it does not harm them but may eventually compete for light. Allow the plant to grow up large trees, such as ash or sycamore, and it will provide nesting and roosting sites as well as berries. The fruits appear in May and June when other berries are scarce and are especially enjoyed by Mistle Thrushes and Woodpigeons. Its value as a nest-site was brought home to me this year when a pair of Spotted Flycatchers nested in one ivy-covered ash tree in my garden and a Stock Dove built its nest in another. Ivy-covered stumps or fence posts make ideal sites for Dunnocks and Wrens. However, do not encourage it to grow on walls as it will damage the mortar.

Laurel *Prunus laurocerasus*
up to 14m (45½ft); chalky to neutral loams; non-native

A clump of laurels or a laurel hedge provides an ideal roosting site for birds in your garden. An old laurel that has become rather leggy should be cut back really hard; it will then sprout vigorously from the trunks to produce thicker growth which will be much better for birds. The early nesting species such as Blackbirds and thrushes favour laurels for their first nest because, being evergreen, the leaves provide a concealed site before the deciduous plants have developed their foliage. Nevertheless, both the leaves and the berries are extremely poisonous.

Privet *Ligustrum vulgare*
up to 5m (16ft); chalky soil; native

If you want to make privet hedges good nest-sites trim them back only a small amount each year until they reach at least 2m (6½ft). Then periodically trim inside the hedge to make good nesting forks. The privet round my garden has been left untrimmed for at least two years and is now ideal for birds. Birds will also eat the black berries without ill effects although they are poisonous to man.

Rhododendron *Rhododendron* spp.
1–10m (3–32½ft); acid soil; non-native

Rhododendrons are mainly of use as roosts once they are mature. They are a non-native

Flowering currant

Honeysuckle

Hawthorn

Ivy

Holly

Laurel

species and therefore do not provide much in the way of insect food, although in snowy weather the clear ground beneath them may be one of the few places where birds can hunt for spiders and insects. Heavy pruning will make the shrub more bushy and improve it for nesting; thickets are often popular with Chiffchaffs. It is not worth planting rhododendrons for birds but do not remove an existing mature clump – it may be the roost of the local Greenfinches.

Rowan or mountain ash *Sorbus aucuparia*
up to 15m (49ft); light soils; native

A rowan in the garden is said to protect the house from evil and the great clusters of red berries provide a splash of colour in early autumn. However, you probably will not enjoy them for long, for they are a great delicacy for all members of the thrush family and also Starlings. Other *Sorbus* species such as white beam also produce good berries for birds.

Spindle *Euonymus europaeus*
5m (16ft); chalky to neutral loams; native

The spindle produces a profusion of pink or orange, four-lobed fruits which thrushes enjoy in spite of them being poisonous to man. The tree is inclined to infestation of black bean aphids which will be popular with insectivorous birds but will not help your bean crop.

Wayfaring tree *Viburnum lantana*
2–6m (6½–19½ft); chalky loams; native

Both wayfaring tree and guelder rose *V. opulus* produce large clusters of berries eaten by thrushes. The flowers which appear in May and June are also very attractive to insects. There is also an evergreen variety *V. tinus* which provides good cover.

Yew *Taxus baccata*
10–25m (32½–81ft); any soil; native

Churchyards are the places to see really mature yews. These trees were no doubt planted to prevent the local peasants from grazing their livestock which would have been poisoned by the foliage; the seeds are also toxic. Song Thrushes and Mistle Thrushes eat the fleshy pink berries but are not harmed as the seeds pass through the gut intact. Yews also provide nest-sites for thrushes, Robins, finches, Dunnocks and Wrens. Sometimes, you may find a Goldcrest's tiny nest hanging from the tips of the branches.

Flowers and weeds for birds

Many flowers that you can grow in your garden have both attractive blossoms and tasty seeds for birds. Sunflowers are the most obvious and will attract finches, tits and Nuthatches. Other seeding flowers include cosmos, china aster, scabious, evening primrose, antirrhinum and phlox. Goldfinches like the seeds of Michaelmas daisies. Their flowers and those of other pink and mauve, late-flowering plants, such as ice plant, buddleia and veronica, are attractive to butterflies.

If you have a large garden and tolerant neighbours a rough patch containing certain weeds is excellent for birds. Thistle, dock, plantain, knapweed, teasel, groundsel, forget-me-not and field poppy are very attractive to the finch family. Stinging nettles are the food plant of red admiral, peacock and small tortoiseshell caterpillars, and since the birds are unlikely to take them all you will also improve your butterfly population. However, you must beware: certain weeds are covered under the Weeds Act 1959 and, as occupier of the land, you can be ordered by the Ministry of Agriculture, Fisheries and Food to prevent them spreading.

Pesticides in the bird garden

The sight of a favourite plant covered in greenfly or a carefully nurtured crop of cabbages riddled with cabbage white caterpillars is enough to cause the mildest person to start spraying madly with an aerosol. Think before you press the button, since the indiscriminate use of pesticides can kill or harm non-pest species as well. For this reason you should always try to be as specific as possible when controlling pests and avoid using general purpose 'cure all' (or 'kill all') products. Toxic chemicals such as DDT, aldrin, dieldrin and heptachlor (all of which are organochlorides and have now been withdrawn from use in gardens) are of this type, and any old stocks of these insecticides should never be used. These persistent chemicals build up in food chains and finally kill or severely affect some of the top predators, particularly birds. Some of the less persistent organochlorides are still available but you should try not to use them if at all possible; use a non-persistent pesticide instead.

Before buying pesticides discover what is affecting your plants; ask an experienced gardener or at your local gardening centre if you are uncertain. Buy a product suited for your problem, but remember that no pesticide is

Privet

Spindle

Rhododendron

Wayfaring tree

Rowan

Yew

23

completely specific so it will inevitably kill some non-pest organisms as well. Use the compound carefully, only where it is needed and follow the manufacturer's instructions precisely. Examine susceptible plants regularly and treat them before the infestation becomes serious. Be especially careful not to contaminate bird-baths, ponds, ditches and streams, since fish are highly susceptible to some chemicals. Do not spray any plants that are in flower as you will kill bees and other pollinating insects. If it is windy be very careful, especially when using herbicides, that the spray does not drift in the wind because you may kill one of your prized herbacious plants.

The following insecticides are fairly harmless to birds and mammals and are not persistent. The names given are the common names of the active ingredients which should be shown on the label. If the active ingredients are not listed do not buy the product. Derris or rotenone (dangerous to fish) and pyrethrum are both naturally occurring substances. The former is made from the roots of a tropical plant *Derris elliptica*, and the latter is prepared from the flowers of a type of chrysanthemum. Organophosporus compounds are extremely toxic but break down quickly and therefore do not build up in the environment. Malathion, bromophos, menazon, pirimiphos-methyl and trichlorphon are all organophos-phates with relatively low toxicity to mammals and birds. They will, however, kill beneficial insects and spiders as well as pest species. Carbaryl and pirimicarb are carbamate compounds that are relatively selective against aphids and capsids which suck plant juices.

Fungicides based on mercury, including calomel (mercurous chloride) and organo-mercury should not be used because they are persistent and some of them can poison wild-life. The fungicides listed in the table below are relatively harmless to wildlife if used correctly with the following provisos: dinocap is danger-ous to fish; copper is not recommended for regular use in orchards as it may kill the invertebrates in the soil, including worms with resulting damage to soil structure; captan, lime sulphur and sulphur can be used both before and after flowering; but thiram should only be used after flowering.

The majority of herbicides are unlikely to cause direct harm to animals but they may destroy their food supplies and alter their habitats. The seeds of weeds such as groundsel, dandelion and nettle provide food for finches; therefore herbi-cides should not be used indiscriminately, particularly if your garden ajoins a hedgerow.

The table below lists the most common garden pests and the recommended treatment which will cause least damage to wildlife.

Insect pests	Treatment
Aphids (greenfly, blackfly)	When exposed, as on pot plants, wash off with soapy water. Otherwise bromophos, derris spray, fenitrothion, malathion (harmful to bees and fish), pirimicarb or pyrethrum. On fruit trees – malathion or pirimicarb.
Blackcurrant gall mite (big bud)	Lime sulphur, sulphur but not on red or white currants and a few varieties of blackcurrant which are susceptible to sulphur.
Capsids } Caterpillars } on fruit trees	Carbaryl, fenitrothion, malathion or pirimicarb
Caterpillars (cabbage white)	Bromophos, derris dust, malathion, pirimiphos-methyl or trichlorphon.
Flies	Pyrethrum.
Red spider mite } Scale insects } on fruit trees	Carbaryl (harmful to bees and fish), fenitrothion, malathion or pirimicarb.
Wasp nests	Derris (harmful to fish).
Woolly aphids	Malathion or menazon

Other animal pests	Treatment
Bullfinch deterrent	Aluminium ammonium sulphate and anthraquinone are relatively non-poisonous but cannot be guaranteed to protect buds in all conditions.

Other animal pests	Treatment
Molluscs (slugs)	Metaldehyde and methiocarb pellets should be carefully covered with a board, brick or flower pot to prevent mammals and birds feeding on them.
Rodents	Break-back traps should be adequately covered so they cannot catch birds. Warfarin should be covered or placed in a pipe out of reach of birds and pets.

Fungicides	Treatment
'Damping off' of seedlings	Captan (harmful to fish), copper or thiram
On fruit: e.g.	Benomyl (harmful to fish), captan, thiram
mould (on strawberry) scab	Benomyl, captan, lime sulphur, sulphur, thiram
On leaves: blight, leaf spots, rusts,	Maneb (harmful to fish and livestock), thiram, zineb
downy mildews (e.g. on lettuce)	Thiram, zineb
powdery mildews	Benomyl, dinocap, lime sulphur, sulphur

Herbicides	Treatment
Lawns:	
daisy and dandelions	2, 4–D (poisonous to fish)
creeping buttercup	MCPA
clovers	Mecoprop, dichlorprop
variety of weeds	Mixture of 2, 4–D with mecoprop or dichlorprop; alternatively dicamba
moss	Lawn sand based on ferrous (not mercurous) chloride or ammonium sulphate. Also prevented by mowing less close, improving drainage, reducing shade or adding limes or other fertilizers.
Newly sown lawns	Ioxynil or morfamquat, once grass is past the two leaf stage.
Newly turfed lawns	No herbicides, except morfamquat, for at least six months
Paths, drives, non-cultivated ground:	
to prevent growth on weed free area for up to a year	Simazine
to control annual weeds	Paraquat – pellets only, liquid is very poisonous.
to control perennial weeds	Dichlobenil, 2,4–D and MCPA. Among established fruit bushes apply dichlobenil in February and March.
In vegetable gardens and flowerbeds:	
to control germinating annual weeds among established plants	Propachlor granules
perennial weeds couch grass	Dalapon alone or with aminotriazole; alternatively bichlobenil. For best results with dalapon apply when grass is growing vigorously and no rain is expected for twelve hours. For couch grass control among fruit trees apply these chemicals in November.
horsetail, coltsfoot, ground elder	Dichlobenil where desirable plants cannot be damaged.
field bindweed or convolvulus hoary cress, dandelions	MCPA or 2,4–D works best when shoots are well grown.

Spring and summer in the garden

It is spring, and suddenly your garden seems full of birds. They are singing, displaying, setting up territories and nest-building. The day length, warmer weather and the increased food supply have triggered off certain hormone changes in the birds and the whole fascinating breeding cycle has started.

Each species carefully times its breeding to coincide with a plentiful food supply. Blue Tits' eggs hatch in mid- to late May when there is a sudden glut of caterpillars, whereas the breeding cycle of a bird of prey, such as the Sparrowhawk, is about three weeks behind. There is then a guaranteed supply of inexperienced young birds about when the Sparrowhawk is busy feeding its own family.

At the onset of spring most birds must set up a territory; some birds such as the Robin and Tawny Owl defend their own patch throughout the winter and are therefore one step ahead. There is much debate over the actual function of a territory and it varies according to the species. To most birds it is a place to woo and mate, build a nest and rear young in relative peace and quiet. With insectivorous birds it is also a defended area where the bird can obtain sufficient food for its mate and young.

The territory is usually established by the male alone and he must let others of his own kind know its boundaries. Most garden birds choose a number of points – a fence, tree or bush – from which they sing. The song-posts are usually distributed round the edge of the defended area and stand out from the surroundings. A Blackbird, for example, will often sing from the edge of a house roof or even from a television aerial.

If another bird of the same species enters a territory it is seen off by the occupant, usually by loud, noisy calling. However, if this is not enough, the owner will use threat displays by trying to make himself look as large and fearsome as possible. Robins blow out their chests and puff out their feathers in order to enlarge their red breast; Great Tits spread their wings downwards and open their bills. This war of nerves goes on until one of the birds gives in by flying away or showing submission. Birds rarely engage in physical combat unless the nest or young are being threatened.

Song is not only used in defence and territory marking but also in courtship. It is a general invitation to any female which happens to hear it. When a hen enters a male's territory he usually displays to her in a threatening manner, but instead of fleeing she stands her ground and adopts a submissive posture, tucking in her head and fluffing out her feathers; persistence usually wins and she is eventually accepted into the area. If, as occasionally happens, two hen birds arrive in a territory, the decision as to which will stay is not made by the cock but by aggressive display between the two hens until one is finally driven out.

Other forms of courtship involve showing-off by the cock or hen, or both: a male Goldfinch swings from side to side flashing the gold on his wings; a cock Whitethroat may offer a piece of grass to his mate for nest-building; and Jackdaws and pigeons 'bill and coo' caressing each other with their bills. Courtship is important as it helps the pair to recognize each other. It also helps form a bond between the two and stimulates mating.

The next step is to choose a nest-site. Usually the male leads in the search but the female has the final say in the matter. Often several nests are started but finally all but one are abandoned and the hen adds the finishing touches with a lining to the nest of her choice.

Nest–sites

In many gardens, particularly new ones where the plants and shrubs have not had time to grow, there may be plenty of food but there is very often a shortage of nest-sites. This problem can be solved for most species by offering them man-made accommodation. You do not have to be a master carpenter to build an adequate nest-box but you must observe certain rules.

Birds are discriminating in their housing requirements and the accommodation must be within a particular size range. There is no point in putting up a large box with a 4cm (1½in) hole and expecting a Blue Tit to nest in it. Most other hole-nesting birds will easily be able to pop through the entrance to threaten and dispossess the occupants. Therefore, before you even pick up the hammer and nails, consider what birds are likely to nest in your garden. It is useless putting up special shells for House Martins if there are no nesting birds nearby.

Garden birds' nesting-sites vary considerably from high in the fork of a tree to low down among herbs on the ground, but basically they can be divided into two sorts – those that nest in holes and those that do not. Tits, Tree and House Sparrows, Starlings and Nuthatches are all hole-nesters and will welcome extra accommodation. However, an entrance hole not more than 2.8cm (1⅛in), will exclude the less desirable House Sparrows and Starlings.

Do-it-yourself nest-boxes

A hole-fronted box can either be cut from an 18–25cm (7–10in) diameter log or a 15cm by 2cm (6in by ¾in) plank about 1.5m (5ft) long. Hardwoods are best but expensive and more difficult to work. A softwood, such as cedar, is ideal as it weathers well; deal or pine can also be used if treated with a preservative to prevent rot. The 2.8cm (1⅛in) hole in the front of the box should be about 2.5cm (1in) down from the top. A perch under the hole is not needed as tits are agile enough to fly straight into the box and it will only give sparrows the chance to sit near the hole and antagonize the occupants. The roof should overhang the hole to keep out rain, and do make sure it is a snug fit as a heavy shower could very easily kill a whole brood. Do not cramp the floor space as a growing brood of about twelve young Blue Tits needs plenty of space (at least 12cm [5in] square). A hole drilled in the bottom of the box is useful for drainage.

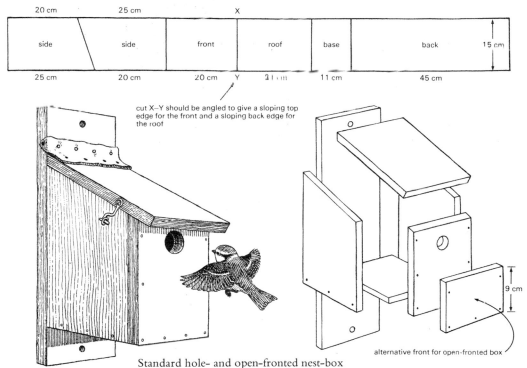

cut X–Y should be angled to give a sloping top edge for the front and a sloping back edge for the roof

alternative front for open-fronted box

Standard hole- and open-fronted nest-box

The box should be fixed between 2–5m (6½–16ft) above the ground to a tree or building and carefully positioned out of reach of cats. It should be sheltered from the wetter more westerly winds and the strong sunlight from the south, and therefore a northerly or easterly direction is most suitable. There must be a fairly clear, but concealed, flight path to and from the box. Also, a branch about 2m (6½ft) away is not only a very useful staging post for the birds, but can be very convenient if you are contemplating any photography. Even though the lid overhangs the box, tilt the whole construction forwards; it can be positioned under a lateral branch at a slope of up to about 45°. It is sensible to fix the box securely but do not worry too much if it swings slightly in the breeze as this is perfectly natural for the birds.

Open-fronted nest-boxes can be made of exactly the same dimensions as the hole-fronted ones but the front panel should be cut down to 9cm (3½ft). This type of box is suitable for Robins, Wrens, Spotted Flycatchers and Pied Wagtails. The positioning of these boxes needs more care: for Robins and Wrens they should be about 1.5m (5ft) off the ground and cunningly hidden in ivy or creeper; flycatchers and wagtails prefer more exposed positions.

Nest-boxes are best fixed into position in the autumn. This gives them a chance to weather and for the birds to become accustomed to them. They may also be used as winter roosting sites. It is, however, always better late than never and I have put up a box in April which was occupied that year by a Blue Tit family.

It is difficult to state categorically how many nest-boxes you should put in a garden. It depends on its size and the availability of natural sites both in the garden and the area around. The easiest way is to start with two or three boxes and slowly add more until some remain unoccupied. Always put up more hole-fronted boxes than open ones.

Your nest-boxes may be made even more acceptable by a neat layer of moss or a few fragments of dried grass on the floor. Remember also that no matter how good your boxes are the birds will add their own personal touch of a nest and lining. Straw and hay, feathers, dogs' and cats' hair, short pieces of cotton, cotton wool and sheep's wool are all excellent nest building materials. It is worth collecting together an assortment in early spring and stuffing it into two mesh bags. Hang one on a branch for tits and Blackbirds and peg the other to the ground for Dunnocks, Wrens and Chaffinches.

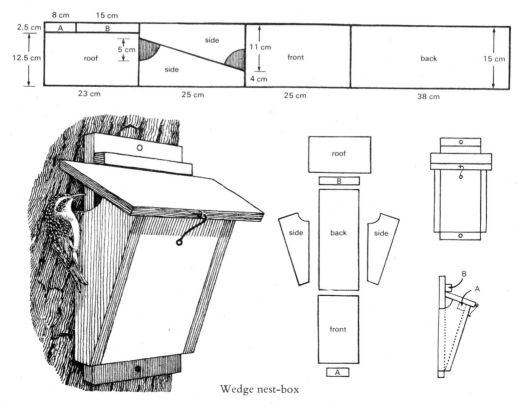

Wedge nest-box

28

Special nest-boxes

Some species need more specialized accommodation and as a general rule these are the less confiding of our garden birds. It is not worth putting up one of these special boxes unless you regularly see the birds in your garden and there is a definite shortage of natural sites for them.

If you have a pair of Treecreepers in your garden it may be worth putting up a wedge-shaped box. It is best situated on the main trunk of a large deciduous or coniferous tree; the height is not important but the box should be out of reach of predators. It may be necessary to chisel away some of the bark to ensure that the box is fitted flush. Alternatively, a piece of bark can be wired to the trunk to provide an artificial crevice.

Tawny Owls will readily take up residence in artificial nest-boxes, particularly in suburban gardens or parks where all the hollow trees and dying timbers have been cleared away. Long, square chimney boxes have considerable conservation value in maintaining or even reclaiming owl populations. The box must be at least 20cm (8in) square and 75cm (30in) long. The bottom can either be made of a piece of perforated zinc or a piece of wood with several drainage holes drilled in it. A layer of peat or sawdust sprinkled on the bottom helps keep the box moderately clean when occupied. These long boxes are difficult to clean out and it is best to fit a small door, 15 by 20cm (6 by 8in), near the base fastened with a hook and eye. The box can be wired to the underside of a lateral branch at an angle of about 30° from the vertical or attached to the trunk at about 45° so that it looks like a broken-off, hollow branch. It is best fixed fairly high up in a mature tree. If you want to check the box the easiest way is to fit a small mirror on a moveable arm above the entrance. But approach an occupied nest cautiously as the birds will often attack intruders including well-meaning birdwatchers.

Special artificial House Martins' nests can be purchased from Nerine Nurseries, Brookend, Wellend, Worcestershire. However, even if you are the most amateur of potters, it is fairly simple to make a clay replica of a nest. The clay, however, must be fired in a kiln to withstand weather. The entrance hole is crescent-shaped and must not be more than 2.5cm (1in) deep in order to keep out sparrows. Fix the nest under the eaves and for best results there needs to be an established colony nearby. The more nests you have the better.

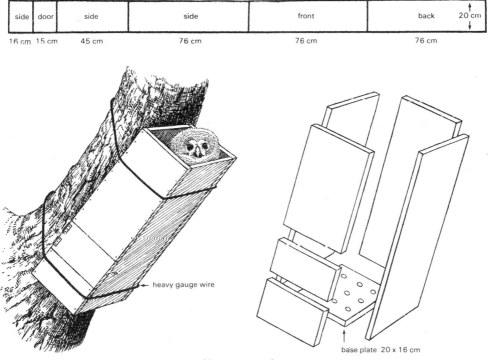

side	door	side	side	front	back	20 cm
16 cm	15 cm	45 cm	76 cm	76 cm	76 cm	

← heavy gauge wire

base plate 20 x 16 cm

Chimney nest-box

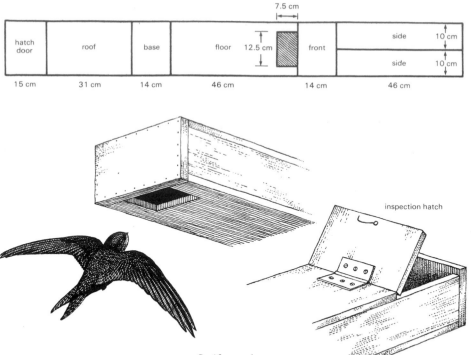

hatch door	roof	base	floor	12.5 cm	front	side	10 cm
				7.5 cm		side	10 cm
15 cm	31 cm	14 cm	46 cm		14 cm	46 cm	

inspection hatch

Swift nest-box

Even if the nest opening is too small to admit a sparrow, a continuous war will still be waged between the two species both over artificial and natural sites. One successful method of putting an end to this is based on the fact that martins are more agile flyers and can approach their nests at a far steeper incline. Strings, not more than 30cm (1ft) long and weighted with a heavy nut or bolt at one end, can be fixed to the eaves with drawing pins about 6cm (2in) apart and 15cm (6in) from the front of the nests. The martins happily fly up to their nests from below unworried by the strings but the sparrows are thoroughly deterred and do not attempt to fly through them.

Swallows do not require such elaborate constructions and small ledges on the inside of a shed or garage are ideal. Swifts can be provided with a place to nest by simply making narrow slits in the eaves to allow access to the roof, or Swift boxes are even better and prevent mess in the loft. These are positioned in place of a brick or piece of wood that has been carefully removed from under the eaves; the nest-box then protrudes with the back of the entry hole flush with the outside brickwork. During the winter, it can be pulled back to block the hole and it should not be pushed out again until the Swifts return in late April; this prevents unwelcome squatters such as sparrows and Starl-

ings. Swifts desert very easily during incubation and so do not disturb them.

Other nest-sites

If you feel that all this carpentry and pottery is quite beyond you, with a little bit of thought and imagination you can still easily help to relieve the avian housing shortage. An old saucepan, kettle or perhaps a flowerpot tucked into the undergrowth may well suit a Robin or a Wren. Half an empty coconut shell tucked into the creeper on the side of the house may entice a Spotted Flycatcher and a piece of sacking nailed to the trunk of a tree may support the beautiful moss and grass nest of a Wren.

Garden sheds provide ideal nest sites, so leave the door slightly ajar during the breeding season or make a small hole in one of the sides. Song Thrushes and Blackbirds may nest in the odd space on a shelf, Swallows may use the eaves and the old piles of pea sticks may house a Wren family. Do ensure, however, that there are no open bags of fertilizer or pesticide lying around as young birds peck at anything in sight. An open can of paint or creosote could become a lethal trap for a young bird making its first intrepid flight.

Never be too tidy in the garden, a brick removed from an old wall may encourage a nesting Pied Wagtail, Spotted Flycatcher or Wren. A pile of branches or twigs is ideal for Dunnocks, Blackbirds and Song Thrushes.

Nests in the garden

If and when the birds nest in your garden leave them alone as much as possible. If you must inspect the clutch make a quick visit every two or three days when the adult bird is not sitting. Be very careful not to leave any signs of your visit such as broken twigs or trodden foliage, as this might well lead predators to the nest. Be particularly careful when the young are almost ready to fly, lifting the lid could well result in an explosion of young fledglings which are not quite ready to leave the nest. If this should happen replace the lid, collect up the young and 'post' them back through the hole and finally plug the entrance with a handkerchief. Unblock the hole about ten minutes later when the whole brood has quietened down.

An unfeathered young bird which has obviously fallen out of a nearby nest should be carefully replaced. If, however, you cannot find the nest sit quietly some distance away and you may see the parents return to feed the rest of the brood. A fully feathered young bird hopping about on your lawn squeaking loudly has not normally been abandoned and it is best to leave it alone. If the fledgling is in an exposed position you can move it into the nearest cover; the parents will soon return with food. In case you are still worried about the youngster, return only after several hours, and if you are certain the bird is still in trouble and is obviously becoming weaker, you must make a decision. The bird can be taken home and placed in a covered box but you must be prepared for a long, messy, time-consuming task which is unlikely to be successful. Never be too eager, however, to take on such work. The younger the bird the more difficult it will be to release it into the wild; you can never hope to give the bird the attention it would receive from its parents and it will have difficulty fending for itself.

Having decided that there is really no alternative, the first thing is to find suitable food for the fledgling. For thrush-sized birds a crushed, soaked biscuit is suitable with a little hard-boiled egg yolk and a few pieces of earthworm. Smaller birds can be fed small insects, caterpillars, ant cocoons, blowfly maggots (obtainable from angling shops) and cut up mealworms. Fragments of tinned dog food are a good substitute for insects but do not agree with all birds. It is best to try a variety of foods first and sort out which suits each bird best. Remember though that all food must be moistened.

Use forceps or tweezers for feeding and push the food well down its throat. (You may find that touching the bill with the forceps is enough to make the bird gape.) If the bird will not open its bill gently force it open with your thumb and forefinger and get someone else to push the food down.

Young birds eat their own weight in a day and should not go without food for more than two hours during daylight. Always leave pots of food and water in the box to encourage the bird to feed itself and keep it in the warm, out of draughts. As soon as the bird can fly, it is best placed in an aviary where it can exercise its wings and practise picking up food from the ground and vegetation. Do not make the bird a pet and only go to it to give it food and water. Release the bird in a safe, secluded area with plenty of food as soon as it is flying well.

Nest-box predators

In country areas weasels can be serious nest predators and many people do not realize what dexterous tree-climbers they can be. However, large metal funnels around the entrance holes of nest-boxes seem to act as fairly successful deterrents. Grey squirrels and Great Spotted Woodpeckers often enlarge the hole of a nest-box in order to reach the young or eggs inside. Special metal plates can be obtained and glued or screwed to the front of the box to help eliminate this. Some predators, however, will even break through the side of the box.

It is not possible to stop Magpies, Jays or crows robbing nests. They are wild birds too and have their place in the community. In all natural systems some creatures prey on others and this helps to control the surplus population – it is called the balance of nature. Imagine the bird population problem in your garden if every nest produced its full quota of young. The food supply could not possibly support them all so some must die to maintain the balance, be it in the bill of a Magpie or by starvation.

The end of the season

Once the breeding season is over clean out all your nest-boxes in order to remove the parasites that have gathered. The remains of old nests may also deter other birds from nesting next year. Shake out the contents and leave the box open in the sun for a short while. Sprinkle moss or dried grass in the bottom of the box if you wish. This may encourage tits or Wrens to use it as a winter roosting site.

Autumn and winter in the garden

The leaves are turning to their autumn shades of reds, browns and yellows; fruits and berries are ripening. The young reared in the nest-boxes are fully fledged and fending for themselves. The plenty of summer has passed and the birds must now prepare to face the hard winter.

Some birds opt out of our cold winter completely and fly south to warmer climates. The gatherings of Swallows on the telegraph wires tells us that autumn is on the way. Their diet, like that of many other summer migrants, is composed entirely of flying insects which are in extremely short supply in the cold weather. They must therefore leave for another summer in the southern hemisphere.

In the Arctic the Waxwings, Fieldfares and Redwings are preparing to leave their breeding grounds. Like the Swallows they too cannot tarry for soon the weather will become totally unsuitable for bird life. All the water and even the ground will freeze and the vegetation will be covered with snow. As daylength shortens there will be insufficient time for the birds to find enough food from the diminishing supply. They must therefore fly south to the more temperate climate of western Europe where they will find fruits and berries in the hedges and woods to tide them over the winter.

Many of our other winter visitors have not come quite so far. The large flocks of Chaffinches, Starlings and Woodpigeons that you see at this time of year are birds that have bred on the Continent and have moved west to take advantage of our milder oceanic climate. The birds that nested in the uplands of Scotland and northern England, such as the Redpolls, also move down to the lowland regions.

The Great Tits that nested in your garden may join up with other tit families and move out into the surrounding woodland. (However, they will all come back into the garden when the weather is really severe to feed on your bird-table.) In the woods they form mixed flocks with other species but each species remains roughly separated within these groups, since they find their various foods in slightly different places. The Great Tits rummage through the undergrowth and leaf-litter; Blue Tits feed high in the branches and the Marsh Tits collect their food from low down on the large boughs.

.Flocks, like breeding colonies, reduce the chance of attack by predators and increase the likelihood of finding a plentiful food supply. Other birds gather together to roost; flocks of finches collect in even larger groups to spend the night in thick evergreens and Starlings will fly up to thirty miles to roost with others of their kind. Even birds which are solitary by day, like the Wren, often crowd together at night in nest-boxes or natural holes for warmth.

At the end of the breeding season, the feathers of adult birds have become very frayed and tattered and therefore most birds moult so that their plumage is in really good condition to conserve as much warmth as possible in the winter months ahead. In addition, on cold nights, the birds fluff out their feathers to trap larger volumes of air between their body and feathers; this gives extra insulation in the same way as a string vest. In most species, the beak and legs lack feathers and therefore heat is lost very rapidly from these surfaces. To reduce this loss a roosting bird sits down on its legs and tucks its bill into the feathers on its back. Birds can survive periods of cold providing they have sufficient food to maintain their body temperature. However, it is not always easy to scratch a living when the ground is frozen and there are less daylight hours for searching, and therefore you can help the birds survive by providing the right food for them.

Feeding the birds

Before you start putting out any food for the birds there are a few simple rules to observe.

October or November is the time to start feeding your birds. There is no need to feed in the spring and summer and it can even be fatal. Nestlings can easily be killed if the adult birds feed them on unnatural foods such as peanuts and white bread, so it is best not to put temptation their way. The only reason for putting out food at this time is to make it easier for you to watch the birds. If you decide to do this then you should only feed with foods that do not harm the young, for example, ant eggs, mealworms, rich fruit cakes or dog or cat food.

It is usually quite adequate to put food out once a day. In the winter, however, birds have to lay down fat reserves during the day as well as filling their crops just before going to roost to provide the energy to keep them warm through the night. In hard weather, the Bullfinch is a most proficient slimmer as on average it loses about half its fat each night. In this case the slimming regimen is a matter of life and death, since if the bird roosts with insufficient fat it will freeze to death. Therefore, in hard weather food should be provided twice a day; in the morning so that the birds can build up their fat reserves, and in the afternoon to allow them to go to roost with a full crop. Once you start putting out food the birds will become dependent on it. If you stop, particularly in the very cold weather, the birds may die of starvation.

Do not put out too much food because if the birds are faced with a surfeit they become lazy. They cease to forage for a wider variety of wild seeds, fruit and insects which would normally be included in their diets. Such deficiencies can reduce the birds' resistance to disease. Also, with time to spare the sparrows will be tempted to rip apart your polyanthus and crocus flowers and the Blue Tits may remove the putty from your window frames to relieve their boredom. The aim should be to attract dozens rather than hundreds of birds and in this way you will avoid killing them with kindness.

It is not sufficient just to throw out a few slices of white bread on the lawn. Unless soaked it could swell up and choke the birds to death and, like man, birds cannot live by bread alone.

Desiccated coconut should be avoided for the same reason and never put out very salty foods, such as salted peanuts, for they could also be fatal. Garden birds find it difficult to get rid of salt since they lack the special salt excreting gland above the eye found in all sea-birds.

The bird food guide

Different groups of birds are adapted to feed on different types of food. The Robin with its thin, delicate bill and long legs is designed to search the ground for insects among the leaf-litter. On the other hand, the Redpoll's shorter legs and stubbier bill are ideal for hanging in the branches and extracting seeds from alder cones. Basically, garden birds can be divided into two groups: the true seed-eaters such as the Greenfinch with its hard bill and the slender, more soft-billed insect-eaters like the Wren.

Natural seeds, fruits and berries provide excellent food for the seed-eater and are the cheapest today when everyone is trying to economize. Every autumn it is well worth gathering hazel nuts, acorns, conkers, sweet chestnuts and beech mast. The chopped kernels can be used either in a feeding-basket or mixed in a bird pudding. Pine cones can be collected when they are still tightly closed and placed on a tray by a radiator to open; the seeds can then be shaken out.

Hips, haws, elder, holly, ivy, rowan and yew berries are the natural foods of the thrushes. Dry the berries in a warm room and then store them in a cool, dry place where the mice cannot get them. Crab apples are also worth gathering.

Bundles of thistle, teasel, ragwort, fat hen, groundsel, redleg, campion and wild grass should be collected once they have seeds. Dry them in the sun before storing in a dry place. Later in the season these can either be hung from branches or stood in the ground for finches.

Not all of you will have the time or the access to areas of countryside where you can go gathering nuts and berries. In this case, the birds' diets can be supplemented with a variety of artificial foods.

In winter, birds need energy-giving foods to keep them warm and therefore fat is important. Large marrow bones, bacon rind, ham skin, and suet, which can easily be obtained from your local butcher, are all energy-giving foods. Suet is also extremely useful for binding together other foods such as stale cake and small seeds which might otherwise be blown away.

Bird puddings can be made for both the insect and seed-eaters and therefore will be suitable for the majority of your garden visitors. There are many variations but the basic recipe is about 8oz (225g) of suet to 1lb (450g) of seed mixture. This can include seeds, stale cake, oatmeal, corn, peanuts and other nuts, dried fruit, cooked rice and spaghetti – you can develop your own special formula. Place a mixture of the dry foods in an aluminium dish, half a coconut shell, small flowerpot or any other suitable mould. Pour the melted fat over this and allow to set before turning out. The pudding can either be placed on your bird-table or, left in its container and hung from a branch or table.

Baked potato and stale cake (particularly stale fruit cake) are other useful foods. Oats, maize flakes and canary seeds are all suitable for the seed-eaters as are sunflower seeds (which can be grown in your own garden). Over-ripe fruit and windfalls are good for thrushes. Crumbled up cheese and bacon rinds are favourites of Wrens, Robins and Goldcrests, and even left-overs from the dog or cat's plate will be welcomed by most insectivorous birds. If you want to hand-tame a Robin, mealworms are a sure way to its heart. These can be bought from pet shops but are expensive; or they can be homebred which requires a certain amount of enthusiasm. Maggots which can be obtained from angling shops are also a treat. However, remember to place both types of larvae (mealworm and maggot) in a straight-sided container before putting them out on the bird-table.

Specially prepared bird foods can be bought and are ideal. Peanuts both whole and shelled are definite winners with all members of the tit family. They are full of protein, excellent cold weather foods and are also much appreciated by many other birds, but if devoured by swarms of marauding sparrows, bird feeding can become extremely costly. An ordinary fresh coconut sawn in half and hung up can also be fed to tits but will always be second choice if there are peanuts about.

If you have any larger birds visiting your garden such as Moorhens, Mallards, Jackdaws, pigeons and gulls, boiled potato peelings and other household scraps are good. All these birds have insatiable appetites and so quantity rather than quality is needed.

Bird-tables

Just as every species prefers particular foods, each one likes to feed in a different part of the garden and in its own characteristic way. The most common place to feed birds is on a bird-table and this can vary from a simple tray to a complex timbered residence. The extremely elaborate ones can be bought from many garden centres and may delight the owners but very often frighten off the more timid species.

A perfectly adequate table can be made from a flat piece of wood, preferably marine ply, with square battens round the edge. I always feel that a roof is unnecessary because the birds seem to prefer an unobstructed field of view when feeding which also enables you to see them much better. A roof will of course partially protect the food from the rain and snow.

The table can be either hung from a branch or attached to a smooth pole; rustic posts should be avoided since they can be easily climbed by cats or squirrels. Squirrels are inveterate bird-table feeders and it is difficult to discourage them. Many ingenious ideas have been tried but the squirrel's acrobatic prowess usually wins. A most effective squirrel barrier can be made by slipping a length of polythene pipe over the pole to within 15cm (6in) of the top. Then a hole is cut in the centre of a large biscuit tin, which is placed onto the pole so that it rests upside down on the top of the piping. Although squirrels can often climb the pole, when they try to reach out to clamber round the biscuit tin, they slide off the smooth piping. Personally, I rather welcome squirrels as bird-table visitors, and have watched them feed regularly at mid-day when the birds have had their fill. They usually come down for a piece of wholemeal bread, then with a clean of the whiskers, they are away back to the woods with their morsel.

The ideal bird-table should be placed about 1.5m (5ft) off the ground in a sheltered position. It should be fairly near a tree or hedge so that the birds can make an inconspicuous approach or beat a hasty retreat; but the cover must not be within easy pouncing range for the local cat.

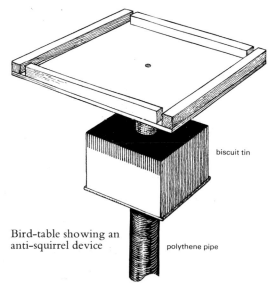

Bird-table showing an anti-squirrel device

biscuit tin

polythene pipe

Bird cake, kitchen scraps, brown bread and seeds are ideal for your table. If it has a roof a seed-hopper can be conveniently hung from the top or an upturned jam-jar suspended just above the top of the table works just as well.

House Sparrows and Starlings are considered nuisances on many bird-tables and there are a variety of feeding devices designed to outwit them ranging from special baskets to coils of wire. However, unless these baskets are suspended on a string at least 1m (3ft) in length so that they swing and spin in the wind, sparrows, which are determined and ingenious feeders, will soon learn to hang from them as well as any tit. Hanging feeders also have two disadvantages: first, the food is only accessible to the most agile species and, secondly, some of the commercially manufactured devices can be dangerous. You must examine them carefully for sharp edges that could cut a bird's feet and for springs that could trap a bird by its wings. A very simple scrap-container can be made from the mesh bags often used for storing onions and carrots. These, however, can become rather unhygienic with decaying fat and in the long run you will find it best to buy a plastic coated scrap basket.

Another extremely useful container is the spiral tit-feeder which is irresistible to tits when full of peanuts. It can be hung either from the bird-table or from a window by means of a suction bracket. For anyone who is confined to one room this can provide hours of endless entertainment; I have even had a Nuthatch feeding from one at my bedroom window. An even simpler feeding device for tits can be made by threading peanuts on a string.

A feeding platform built out from a window-sill is an excellent idea for people with small gardens or living in flats. I have received letters from people living in high-rise buildings who are regularly feeding Blue and Great Tits over 25m (80ft) above ground; I have also heard of nest-boxes being used in similar positions. It is best to choose a sheltered side of the house away from both direct sun and strong winds when siting the platform or box.

Many birds, however, are reluctant to feed from a table and are not adapted to perform aerobatics from a hanging basket. For birds such as Dunnocks and Pied Wagtails it is best to sprinkle some seeds and scraps on the ground. It is most important to feed on the ground only in an open area well away from cover as these species are even more vulnerable to the feline predator that may be lurking behind a bush.

In some places rats may be attracted to bird food and it is important to put out only as much food as the birds will eat. Remove un-eaten food and collect up all mouldy or rotting remains. You should also move your bird-table at least once during the winter. Regularly scrape it clean, and if droppings have accumulated on the ground clear them away and burn them. At the end of the season when you take your bird-table down, wash it with 10 per cent ammonia solution; you can also cleanse the area around the table with the same solution to destroy any parasite eggs.

The shyer visitors

Some birds are usually too shy to come near a bird-table. They normally manage to find food but when there is thick snow or frost they do need help. After a heavy snowfall, a cleared patch of earth in a sheltered part of your garden will reveal insects and spiders which provide a welcome supplement for many insect-eating birds. Suet pushed into the cracks in the bark or a large piece of it wired to the bough of a tree is suitable for all members of the woodpecker family. A special woodpecker feeder can be made by drilling 3cm (1in) holes into a small log. Each hole is then filled with suet and the whole device hung in a tree.

In very heavy snow the thrushes suffer, and in particular Redwings, which soon die of starvation. This is the time to clear out any apples that are beginning to go bad; use up the crab apples you gathered in the autumn or ask your local greengrocer for a box of rotting fruit. This should be scattered well away from the house. Acorns can also be sprinkled on the ground for Jays or pigeons. It is worth covering over the feeding area with a sack at night if it looks like snow; it can then be easily removed in the morning with the snow on top.

In such bad conditions, leave the door of your garden shed slightly ajar, since Wrens rarely visit bird-tables but love to search in the odd nook or cranny for spiders and insects.

Jackdaws and Magpies are self-sufficient creatures and usually manage to find food in the coldest of weather. They watch out for birds that are weak or dying and feed on the carrion. They will even wait near a bird-table and dive onto the resident birds as they fly off with food in their bills, harassing them until they drop their meal.

Once the last frost of April has passed there is no longer any need to feed. In spring, most of your bird-table birds begin searching for animal foods such as caterpillars, spiders, worms and other insects. They will now help you by destroying hordes of insect pests far more safely than any toxic chemical.

Watching more closely

Your garden should now be a haven for birds – but what can you do next? The joy and excitement of birdwatching even for the beginner is that there is always something new to see or hear. It is unnecessary to be an expert at bird identification to appreciate the acrobatics of a feeding bird, be it a Marsh or Willow Tit. The appeal of birdwatching as a hobby is that it offers something for everyone.

The most basic form of birdwatching is to keep a list of the species you see in the garden. I have recently moved into a new house and at present my garden bird list stands at only twenty-eight species but I am .always on the lookout for newcomers. Even a common bird is a celebrity when it first appears in your garden.

It is more interesting to keep a detailed record of your garden birds, noting the arrival and departure dates of summer and winter visitors. You will soon discover that your resident birds also show seasonal movements in and out of the garden. The longer you keep the diary the more you will learn from it as annual patterns begin to emerge. Each year you will be able to predict the arrival of your Spotted Flycatcher or the departure of your Swallows with increasing accuracy. If you also keep some weather records you will discover its effects on bird movements.

Bird song is a fascinating topic of study and one that I still have not successfully mastered. The easiest way to learn is to go out with an expert. However, if you are in the garden and hear a bird singing, stand still and see if you can spot the bird itself. For some species, especially the warblers, song is the best method of identification. On a February or March evening it is well worth listening to some bird recordings of summer migrants to get to know their songs before they arrive.

Different species sing at different times of the year so keep a monthly account of when you hear the songs of your garden residents. You will find that some species sing mainly in the spring, whereas others have a burst of autumnal song and a few sing every month of the year. At least once every spring, however much you enjoy your sleep, you must stay up late or wake up early to hear the dawn chorus; the sheer cacophony of sound never ceases to amaze me. If you are a regular night owl or early bird try to discover which species are the first songsters as the season progresses.

The feeding times of different species are useful to record. You may find that your bird-table is plagued with sparrows in midmorning whereas the Great Tits and Robins feed earlier. It may then be possible to work out the best times to put out food.

Food selection experiments, if carried out over a fairly long period, will tell you what kind of food to put out on your table to attract a particular species. These tests need not be at all complicated; if you place some different foods, such as seed, bacon rind, suet, peanuts and brown bread, in similar containers on the table, you will be able to record how many times certain species visit each container. The birds will similarly select the natural foods in the garden, and by watching regularly you can discover which berry-bearing shrubs, for example, the Blackbirds prefer. Are they the same variety as those eaten by the Song Thrush or Robin?

Personally, I find bird behaviour and ecology the most fascinating topics of birdwatching, and a bird-table is an ideal study area. Each bird has its own way of feeding and its anatomy has evolved for maximum efficiency. The heavy bill of the Greenfinch is ideal for cracking large seeds, while the short, strong legs of the Blue Tit enable it to hang upside down from a coconut. The more you watch birds the more you will appreciate that every part of them is designed for their particular way of life.

While observing the birds on your table you will soon notice that there is a definite social structure. Certain species are dominant and within each species there is a 'boss bird'. Each kind of bird has a different form of aggressive display. If you watch closely you will see how a species emphasizes certain characteristics of its shape and plumage. It is also interesting to look at an individual being threatened and you will notice that it is trying to conceal the characteristics the aggressor is displaying, in an attempt at appeasement. The behaviour patterns of birds are complicated but they conform to a regular sequence; work these out by drawing simple sketches or taking photographs.

A good bird gardener should keep a record of the species nesting in the garden and of their sites. This helps to give a rough guide to the positioning of more boxes, which ones to move and which shrubs need pruning. When you do find a nest do not check it too often and then only when the bird is away. It is interesting to note the size of the completed clutch and the approximate date when incubation started, and you need not disturb the bird to discover this. While the bird is laying it will only visit the nest briefly, but once it starts to incubate it will sit steadily, leaving only for short periods. From this you can work out when the young are expected to hatch. These can be counted in the nest but it is not until they are feeding round the garden that the true success rate will be known. If you get a very high mortality rate for a clutch, it is best to check that the nest-box is not too exposed. The problem could be that either rain is getting into the nest-box or it is getting too much direct sun, causing the young to die of chilling or heat-stroke respectively.

The breeding season is also a good time to try to plot bird territories. A Robin occupies an area of about 0.5 hectares (1 acre), a Great Tit one hectare (2½ acres) and a Tawny Owl anything from 4–40 hectares (10–100 acres) – the size depending very much on the richness of the habitat. Few gardens, therefore, are likely to contain more than a single territory. However, you are likely to have a territory boundary running through your garden. On a rough sketch map of the garden mark the spots where a bird is seen regularly singing; Robin, Black-bird or Great Tit have strong territorial instincts and are good species to study. Also mark on your map where you see two birds displaying or singing to each other. A bird chasing another will stop at its boundary which will be another point to mark on the territory map, and gradually a boundary line will become apparent.

If you ever wish to measure the population of birds in an area, this can be done by plotting the territories in a similar way. Select a larger area – a group of gardens, a local park or nearby farmland. Visit it regularly during the breeding season, preferably first thing in the morning, and mark on the map every bird seen, noting especially if it is singing. Two birds singing simultaneously or having a boundary dispute are extremely useful observations. After a series of visits (the more the better, but at least eight will be necessary) plot every observation of each species on a master map. You will find they form a series of clusters each of which represents a territory.

Useful equipment

As you become more interested in birdwatching you will want a pair of binoculars. There is a vast assortment on the market, so which should you choose? I think the most important factor is size and weight, having just recently changed a large, heavy pair which I rarely bothered to take out with me, for a much lighter pair. As far as cost is concerned you get what you pay for. However, as a pair of binoculars is likely to last you a lifetime I would advise anyone to buy the best quality they can afford.

There are two sizes of binoculars used mainly by birdwatchers: 8 x 30 or 40 and 10 x 50; the first number gives the magnification and the second is the diameter of the large object lens. By dividing the magnification into the diameter you obtain the exit pupil diameter which gives you an indication of the light-gathering potential. A value of 3.75mm is sufficient but over 4mm is preferable to enable good views of birds. Binoculars with a magnification of 8 x 30 or 8 x 40 are very suitable for watching your garden birds or for a walk in a wooded area. Buy a pair with larger magnification (10 x 50) if you spend a lot of time birdwatching on reservoirs, estuaries or at the sea, where you are looking at birds from a great distance.

When buying your binoculars choose a pair that is focussed by a main central wheel and has a separate adjustment for one of the eye pieces; this compensates for any difference in focussing between your eyes. You must test the binoculars outside the shop. Check that they feel comfortable in your hands and focus them on a distant object such as a mast or aerial. Make sure that there are no distortions or coloured edges round the image; your eyes should not feel strained in any way. It is also important to check that the binoculars focus on near objects down to about 6m (20ft) away.

If you wear glasses, it is best to remove them or push them up when using binoculars, or better still, you can purchase a pair specially designed for use with or without glasses.

Photographing birds

A camera is by no means as essential as a pair of binoculars but if you already have one why not try taking some shots of the birds feeding on the bird-table or bathing in your pond? An ordinary 'Instamatic' camera is not really suitable as it will not focus close enough and does not have a fast enough shutter speed for the quick movements of a bird. The best type of camera for bird photography is a 35mm, single lens reflex camera and if it does not have a built-in light meter you will need to buy a separate one. A standard 50mm lens is adequate but you will also need a good, rigid tripod and a pneumatic release. It is best to start with a medium speed film, 125 ASA black-and-white or 64 ASA colour; a faster film may be necessary on an overcast day; if you are in any doubt ask at your local photographic shop.

A few days before taking your photographs, put up a short pole with a dummy camera on the top near your bird-table or pond. Do not desert your garden completely at this time – walk about at the far end away from the bird-table. The birds will soon become accustomed to both you and the camera.

On a suitable bright, sunny day set up your camera and tripod in place of the dummy camera and with luck the birds should be none the wiser. Place the camera about 60cm (2ft) away from the table. Then set the shutter speed to not less than 1/60 second; a faster speed will help to stop any small movements. The reading on your light meter will tell you the combination of the shutter speed and aperture (the

'f' stop) appropriate to the amount of light on the subject and you can set your camera accordingly; it is best to take several shots and then to experiment with various readings. Link up the pneumatic release and position yourself behind a suitable bush or even inside the house if your table is near the window. Be patient, do not release the shutter as soon as a bird has landed, but wait until it is in exactly the right position. When the camera clicks the bird will probably fly off; you can then wind on the film and reset the shutter. The birds should be used to you walking round the garden and will soon return to the table ready for your next shot.

If you become interested in this aspect of birdwatching you will need to buy a lens with a longer focal length; a 135mm is ideal. This will allow you to move the camera about 1.5m (5ft) away from the subject. An alternative way to increase the focal length of your lens is to buy a x2 converter. This is an additional lens which goes between your standard lens and camera body and doubles the focal length. For example it will turn your standard 50mm lens into 100mm. Although this is a cheaper alternative it does have certain technical disadvantages.

Do not be tempted to try to photograph birds at the nest. You might well cause the birds to desert and it is illegal to photograph specially protected species, like the Barn Owl or Kingfisher, at the nest without a licence from the Nature Conservancy Council. It requires very little skill or patience to take a nest shot, and these photographs tend to be dull and often the bird is ill at ease. It may take much longer to get a good shot of a bird feeding on the table, bathing or performing an aggressive display but, in the long run, you will have a much more interesting picture of a bird behaving naturally.

In this section I have tried to whet your appetites with a few of the more interesting aspects of birdwatching. There are many books which will provide much more information and some of these are listed on page 122.

The following section of the book will illustrate both in colour and black-and-white forty-nine common garden birds and provide brief notes about their activities in your garden.

The garden birds

Robin

The Robin (*Erithacus rubecula*) certainly tops the popularity poll among garden birds but it is not the most common. Over the last hundred years the British population has remained relatively constant around the five million mark whereas the Wren numbers twice that amount.

The Robin has always been a favourite of man; in folklore, it is said to have plucked a thorn from Jesus's crown, piercing its own breast and the stain remains as a badge of honour. Nowadays, it is a popular subject for Christmas cards, not only being associated with the crucifixion but also as a symbol of warmth and friendship.

Every gardener looks out for his local Robin. Perched on a spade or wheelbarrow it scans the newly turned earth for worms and larvae. On the bird-table it is fond of crumbs but mealworms and cheese are its favourites. The Robin is one of the easiest birds to tame and unfortunately its over-inquisitive nature often causes it to take fatal risks with cats or even machinery.

It is only in Britain that the Robin is such a companion to man. On the Continent, it is a shy, retiring woodland bird better known for its ticking alarm call.

The Robin is remarkable among songbirds in holding a territory throughout the year. During the breeding season both sexes ward off intruders. In the autumn, the pairs split up; the males and females stake out independent areas which they defend by singing and displaying round the boundaries. Bird-tables act as a powerful attraction to neighbouring Robins and therefore are good places to watch the Robin's threat display. The owner puffs out his chest to show off his red breast to best advantage. This sight is usually sufficient to frighten off the stranger.

The bird's actions are instinctive. A stuffed Robin or even a bunch of red feathers evokes a threatening display whereas a bird with a brown coloured breast elicits no reaction. What is the purpose of this fierce territoriality? A Robin hunts by dropping from a perch; its foraging would be far less successful if it was being constantly pestered by another bird.

Robins pair up as early as December – long before the traditional Valentine's Day. At first the hen is attacked but, persistent to the last, she is eventually accepted into the territory. In its typical woodland habitat the hen builds the nest low in a natural crevice, while in a garden, kettles, cans and buckets make excellent substitutes. Throughout the incubation the hen is fed by the cock. The speckled brown young are often misidentified for they lack the red breast and this allows them to remain in their parents' territory without being attacked. At the end of July, when they moult into their adult plumage, they must leave and find a territory of their own.

Dunnock

The sombre colouring and habit of skulking, mouse-like in the undergrowth makes the Dunnock (*Prunella modularis*) an easily overlooked bird. To many it is just another sparrow and some people still stubbornly call it the Hedge Sparrow. In fact the Dunnock is in no way related to the Tree or House Sparrow; it has a different shaped bill and totally different behaviour patterns.

Spring is one of the best times to watch this shy, secretive bird when several individuals display together on a lawn. One wing is quickly spread and lifted above the back in a quivering movement and, at the same time, the Dunnock utters its squeaking call. In Sussex and Surrey, this courtship display has led to the use of the colloquial name, shuffle-wing.

The Dunnock is an extremely adaptable bird and can be found in a wide range of habitats; it can scrape a satisfactory living even on the bleak Scottish moors or on wind-swept Hebridean islands. Gardens are one of its favourite haunts where it can find plenty of small seeds and insects at the bottom of hedges and among the flowerbeds. It is a regular visitor to the bird-table but always feeds on the ground beneath – gathering the spoils that fall from the rich man's table. However, Dunnocks can be most aggressive; one cold snowy day I watched a Dunnock attack and eventually kill another Dunnock. There is no easy explanation for this extreme behaviour.

In spring, bushes and hedges in the garden provide ideal cover for nesting but these birds have also been known to use old nests of Swallows or thrushes The males are often promiscuous, leaving each female to build her own neat nest of moss and grass and incubate the sky blue eggs. Once the eggs have hatched the cock takes his share in parental responsibility and helps to feed the young.

Cuckoos often choose Dunnocks' nests as a place to lay their eggs. A survey by the British Trust for Ornithology showed that the Dunnock was third in the league table of popular hosts – only the Reed Warbler and Meadow Pipit were more frequent foster parents.

Birdwatchers hardly bother to give this insignificant little bird a second glance and despite its abundance little is known about its movements. In winter, our British population is joined by birds from the Continent. However, we still do not know how many of our birds migrate south for the winter or the extent of this migration.

Wren

In legend, the Wren (*Troglodytes troglodytes*) is known as the king of the birds and despite its size it has always attracted man's attention. This tiny, brown bird played a part in druidical rites and in modern times was featured on the farthing which has since been withdrawn.

A recent survey showed that the Wren was the most common nesting bird in Britain and Ireland, with a population of about ten million. The Wren's ancestors came from America and invaded the Old World during the Ice Age. The individuals that settled on the Outer Hebrides, Shetland and St Kilda became three separate races.

In Britain, no bird is more widely distributed than the Wren. Although common in our gardens, hedges and woods, its home stretches from the coombes of Devon to the moors of Shetland; on seacliffs it is found nesting alongside the Puffins, while up in the mountains grouse are its neighbours.

One of the Wren's most characteristic features is its incessant activity, scurrying along a hedge in search of likely prey. It feeds almost entirely on insects and spiders but will turn to seeds in winter when animal food is scarce. It is perfectly adapted to hunt its prey in the tiniest nooks and crannies. Its thin, sharp beak is ideal for probing into cracks, while its strong legs enable it to cling upside down like a tit or climb a tree like a Treecreeper. The males will hunt among the leaves of small trees taking caterpillars in the same way as Willow Warblers. The female, which is more secretive, is less likely to venture far from the ground. The Wren is not a frequent visitor to bird-tables but in severe weather it will take cheese and scraps from the ground.

The Wren's size and timid appearance belie its true character. The cock is extremely aggressive and is seldom silent. His amazingly loud, vehement call is used in defence of his territory of about 0.5 hectares (one acre) and can be heard from 600m (650yd). Some of the notes are of such high frequency that they are inaudible to the human ear.

In spring, the cocks are busy building up to ten domed-shaped nests of grass, leaves or moss. They sometimes use open-fronted nest-boxes, or else a few dead leaves poked into a likely corner may persuade them to build there. The male entices the hen into his territory with a warbling courtship song after which she selects a well-hidden nest and adds a feather and down lining. Cock Wrens are not the most faithful of partners; where food is plentiful they may have up to six mates in one season. The hen incubates the eggs but the cock helps to feed the young.

In winter, Wrens roost together in old nests or nest-boxes for warmth. Cold weather can cause dramatic mortality, since the population today is ten times greater than in 1964 which followed two hard winters.

Goldcrest

The Goldcrest (*Regulus regulus*) is well known as Britain's smallest bird and, as you would expect for a bird of such diminutive size, it can be infuriatingly difficult to see. It is far easier to detect by ear; listen beneath a yew or ornamental conifer in the garden and you may well hear its thin, penetrating 'si-si-si' call as it feeds high among the branches. Sit and wait, and you may catch a glimpse of this tiny, warbler-like bird as it hovers out to catch a fly or hangs upside down, as agile as a tit, delicately removing insects with its needle-sharp beak.

Conifer forests are the typical habitat of the Goldcrest. The birds move into the new plantations when the trees are eight or nine years old. They soon outnumber Chaffinches and Willow Warblers and, by the time the plantation is about forty years old, Goldcrests and Coal Tits are by far the most common birds. In Ireland, it is a bird of the sessile oakwoods, but in Britain it only moves into this habitat when numbers are very high. Goldcrests often breed in large gardens or churchyards where there are mature yews or conifers.

In spring, the cock Goldcrest courts his mate by spreading his crest to reveal a fiery red streak down the centre. Together they build a hammock-like nest of moss, lichen and cobwebs, suspended from the tip of a high branch where it is safe from all but the most deft of predators. The pair often rear two and some-times three broods in a season; such high productivity makes for good sense when a species is so vulnerable in hard weather. Frost and snow can make the Goldcrests' insect food-supply virtually unobtainable, but still these independent little birds rarely visit the bird-table. If you have any Goldcrests in your garden some grated cheese sprinkled under the conifers is a most welcome supplement to their diet.

Some Goldcrests, despite their light weight (a Goldcrest is about half the weight of a Blue Tit) migrate south for the winter. Those that remain, join up with parties of tits feeding in the hedgerows and deciduous woods and even in the kale fields.

Our resident population is joined by winter visitors from northern Europe and I cannot help but marvel at the stamina of this small bird. In September, I have walked along the beach at Minsmere in Suffolk and seen large numbers of Goldcrests and the occasional Firecrest, a close relative, flying just above the waves and dropping thankfully into the tamarisk bushes on the dunes after their exhausting journey across the North Sea.

Great Tit

A strange, unfamiliar call in the garden is almost bound to be a Great Tit (*Parus major*). A detailed study of this tit's song distinguished forty different calls from a single bird. However, its most familiar call of 'teecher teecher' is heard from autumn through to the spring and gives the bird its local name, saw-sharpener.

The Great Tit is the largest of the British tits and is easily recognized by its yellow breast and long black central band; the male has a wider, more distinct band than the female. In its natural woodland habitat, it feeds mainly on the ground or low in the bushes where it takes insects, but it also uses its strong beak to crack hazel and beech nuts.

This species is normally the dominant member of the tit family when it comes to sharing a bird-table. It will feed on a nut-basket with its mate but to all other intruders it aggressively spreads its wings and tail and opens its beak.

The Great Tit's ingenuity – almost akin to intelligence – makes this bird such an attractive bird-table visitor. By trial and error it can be taught to operate a system of levers and pulleys in order to obtain a peanut reward. However, its cunning is not always associated with man's artificial feeding devices: 200 years ago Gilbert White, the famous naturalist from Selborne, watched a Great Tit draw straws out of a thatch and eat the flies it had disturbed. There are even stories of a mathematical Great Tit which was trained to reply to pencil taps on a table with the same number of taps with its beak – surely this must have been an avian prodigy.

In spring, Great Tits are catholic in their choice of nest-site and any hole will suffice; hole-fronted nest-boxes are readily accepted. A Great Tit's nest should be a welcome sight to any gardener as the birds feed their young on protein-rich caterpillars, particularly the varieties that devastate fruit trees. It has been estimated that a pair of Great Tits will collect 7–8 000 caterpillars while feeding a brood of young.

Once the fledglings are independent of their parents, adults and first-year birds alike feed in flocks with other species of tits. At first they roost together in dense shrubs, but, with the onset of winter, their roosting habits change. They prefer to nestle singly in a crevice or a hole in a tree, the new site offering greater protection from the cold.

C.F. Tunnicliffe

Blue Tit

Performing aerobatics on a hanging coconut or stealing cream from a milk bottle, tom tit, or more correctly the Blue Tit (*Parus caeruleus*), is one of our best known and best loved garden birds. However, do you know how many Blue Tits are visiting your bird-table? At a garden in Oxford adjoining some woodland well over 100 birds fed at a table in a single morning.

Despite its charm and sprightliness the Blue Tit does not have an entirely spotless record. In 1837, Yarell, in his *History of British Birds*, noted that a bounty was paid by churchwardens for Blue Tits' heads and in one parish seventeen dozen tom tits' heads were collected. Even today they are sometimes considered a serious pest in commercial orchards. Their milk bottle opening ability can also become a nuisance, and in a village where I used to live the engine of the milk float had to be left running to keep the tits at bay.

In certain years when large numbers cross from northern Europe, there have been outbreaks of Blue Tits tearing wallpaper and eating putty. The most probable reason is that the birds are finding easy meals at a nearby nut-basket or bird-table and their physical hunger is therefore satisfied long before their food-searching urge is exhausted. Their hunting urge is thus fulfilled by other destructive activities.

Nuisances apart, anyone who puts up a nest-box hopes that it will be occupied by a Blue Tit. It need not be an elaborate box providing there is sufficient floor-space to raise the vast family. The Blue Tit happily nests in inverted plant pots, hollow posts and even letter-boxes. This species lays one of the largest clutches of any British bird, averaging thirteen, and has been known to hit a record nineteen. The total clutch may amount to 150 per cent of the hen's weight and a plentiful supply of food is therefore crucial and courtship feeding by the male may have a practical as well as ritualistic function.

In woods, laying is so timed that hatching coincides with the time when caterpillars are at their most plentiful. Parent birds have been known to make 1 000 feeding visits in one fifteen to sixteen-hour day. The birds are unlikely to be able to find enough food in gardens unless there are large trees about, particularly oaks, and very often half the brood will die. If you see your Blue Tits collecting greenfly off the roses, the birds are in trouble as it takes several minutes to gather a caterpillar's worth of greenfly.

Of course it would be totally impossible for all young Blue Tits to survive – we would be overrun by them. In fact, a fairly constant population is maintained as 50 per cent of the adults die each year and, on average, one young per pair survives the winter to replace the missing adult.

Coal Tit

The Coal Tit (*Parus ater*) is best recognized by the conspicuous white patch on the nape of its neck and its small size. Normally a bird of coniferous woodlands, it is quite content in gardens if there are some cedars, yews or ornamental cypresses. Its thin, fine bill is an ideal tool for excavating the small insects or larvae from pine needles or crevices in the bark.

Life in the winter is hard for the Coal Tit and a species study revealed that on average one bird searched 1 100 trees in a nine-hour day. Therefore, it is hardly surprising that Coal Tits often supplement their natural winter food with peanuts or fat from bird-tables; even if they have to compete with the more aggressive Blue and Great Tits. However, if you watch closely you will notice that there is a subtle difference in their behaviour. The larger tits eat the nuts straight from the basket or fly off with a large piece to eat on a nearby twig. The Coal Tit, however, dashes away with its prize to store the food in a flowerbed or in a crack in a tree trunk.

Coal Tits nest near to the ground in rotten stumps and their preference for conifers is somewhat surprising since in broadleaved woodland they lay more eggs and rear more young. It is presumed that the Coal Tit has adapted to life in the pine forests in order to avoid competition with the bigger Willow and Marsh Tits which take similar food and use the same nest-sites.

Marsh Tit

The Marsh Tit (*Parus palustris*) is not a brightly coloured bird but all through the year it gives an impression of being meticulously well-groomed and elegant. It is a rural bird occasionally visiting country bird-tables and, as it is a sedentary species, it stores much of its food for times of need. This bird is mainly found in broadleaved woods where it can be extremely difficult to see scurrying low in the bushes. Perhaps the best way to locate a Marsh Tit is to listen for its characteristic 'pitchew' call, or you may be lucky to spot a few birds searching along a track for grain put out for Pheasants.

The name Marsh Tit is somewhat misleading as more often than not this bird is found in dry areas. However, the name was established before the Marsh Tit had been separated from the very similar Willow Tit which is fond of swampy ground.

The Marsh Tit is more restricted in its range than the rest of our British tits – only infrequently has it been recorded nesting north of the border and there are no breeding records of it in Ireland.

Outside the breeding season the Marsh Tit is less gregarious than the other tits and often feeds in groups of two or three on honeysuckle berries and seeds of marsh thistle or knapweed, as well as insects.

Long-tailed Tit

The tiny, delicate Long-tailed Tit (*Aegithalos caudatus*) is only distantly related to the *Parus* group of tits – the Great, Blue, Coal and Marsh Tits. Its nesting habits distinguish it from all *Parus* tits where the female builds the nest alone in a hole.

The Long-tailed Tit's nest is the most elaborate architectural achievement of any British bird. Both the male and the female may start building it in early March and the whole structure can take over three weeks to complete. The 10cm (4in) dome is built of intertwined moss, hair and cobwebs with an outer rendering of grey lichen and is usually found in a gorse or thorn bush or a thick hedge. However, some beautifully camouflaged nests are sometimes built high in an exposed fork of a lichen-covered tree. This is the traditional site for Scandinavian Long-tailed Tits and it has been suggested that our British tit is branching out into a new nesting habitat of bushes and shrubs.

A lining of over 2000 feathers is added to the basic structure; ten to twelve eggs are laid, and by the time the incubating hen has settled herself on top there is very little room. Her head and tail can sometimes be seen corking the entrance, and congestion can become even worse when the cock decides to roost in the nest as well. The breeding success of Long-tailed Tits is low and often you may see three or four adult birds feeding the same young. These extra helpers are bereaved parents from another nest.

Despite their fluffy appearance, these tiny insectivorous birds are very susceptible to the cold and up to 80 per cent of the British population can be wiped out in a hard winter. Groups of five to ten birds often roost together in a dense thicket, huddled in a ball to conserve heat.

The Long-tailed Tit is not a common bird-table visitor, although I have regularly watched a party of five feed on fat and dog food in a sheltered Sussex garden. Recently, they have nested in the London parks, substituting tissue paper for the more usual external nest decoration of lichen.

If you want to watch Long-tailed Tits, your best chance is to visit the local woods in winter and listen for the thin 'zi-zi-zi' contact calls high in the branches. Often a party of about twenty can be seen hanging upside down feeding at the tips of the branches or quickly flitting in a follow-my-leader fashion through the trees. These birds stay together throughout the winter and each flock remains within the same part of the wood which they defend against all other parties of Long-tailed Tits. In spring, the members of each flock nest in this same area.

Tree Sparrow

The Tree Sparrow (*Passer montanus*) is far more common than most people realize, but, being less dependent on man and his activities than the ubiquitous House Sparrow it tends to pass unnoticed. Take a close look at the next flock of sparrows you see in the country and you may notice several much neater, slimmer birds – Tree Sparrows. The cock and hen Tree Sparrow are indistinguishable; they are similar to a cock House Sparrow but have a chestnut cap and a black spot on the cheek. Their presence is most easily detected by their higher pitched chirrup and their distinctive flight call, a harsh 'keek, keek'.

In Britain, the Tree Sparrow is a much shyer, less bumptious bird than its common cousin and more rural in its choice of habitats. It comes to bird-tables in large, secluded gardens but avoids competition with House Sparrows by feeding later in the day. The two species do feed together on stubble but the House Sparrow takes grain while the Tree Sparrow eats many more insects and weed seeds.

In the Far East where the House Sparrow is absent, the Tree Sparrow fills the niche that is occupied by the former elsewhere. It lives in close association with man, breeding in the houses and reaching similar pest proportions. Also, on St Kilda, where the House Sparrow has never bred, the Tree Sparrow lived in the village but soon disappeared once the island was evacuated.

Tree Sparrows are gregarious birds at all times of the year and prefer to nest in colonies. Holes in old hollow trees (such as pollarded willows) haystacks or farm buildings make ideal nest-sites. They do use nest-boxes, especially if there are several in the area, and being slimmer than House Sparrows they can enter boxes designed for tits and oust the rightful tenants. These birds have even been known to build at the bottom of occupied rooks' nests where they feed on the scraps dropped by their unsuspecting hosts.

The Tree Sparrow is most common in eastern Britain, thinning out as one moves west, and it has been suggested that its presence may be associated with areas of low rainfall. Outside the main range its distribution is coastal; this is perhaps a result of birds that have wintered in coastal flocks and have remained to breed. Over the years, the Tree Sparrow's population has fluctuated widely for inexplicable reasons. Until twenty years ago, many colonies nested along the east coast of Scotland but then suddenly disappeared. Now, they are gradually spreading back into these former haunts.

Chaffinch

The Chaffinch (*Fringilla coelebs*) is one of the most common woodland birds and its population has been estimated at around the seven million mark. The Chaffinch and the Blackbird therefore dispute the position as our second most abundant birds.

Fearless and cheeky, the cock Chaffinch is one of our gayest garden birds; the hen has similar markings but is a duller olive-brown colour. It is almost as numerous in gardens as in broadleaved woods provided there are plenty of mature trees on which it can feed.

The Chaffinch, with its long but stout, multipurpose bill is the least specialized of all our finches in its feeding habits. It feeds on both insects and seeds and as its name implies had its heyday prior to automated combine-harvesting. The corn was threshed by hand and large flocks would feed on the seeds among the chaff. Its population declined during the 1950s with the use of toxic chemicals particularly as seed-dressings.

The Chaffinch is a sedentary bird and few move more than 8km (5 miles) from their birthplace. They are territorial and the area defended may range from 1 sq km to over 3 hectares ($\frac{1}{4}$ to over 8 acres). The cock returns to his old territory in mid-February and advertises his presence by singing loudly from the tops of trees and bushes.

The Chaffinch's song is a sequence of notes ending with a flourish, but individuals' songs differ slightly from one another. Where populations are separated by a geographical barrier, such as a river or strip of unsuitable terrain, the differences are far greater. Thus, the Chaffinch's song varies in different regions in the same way as human dialects. The reason for this is that the song is partly innate and partly learnt. A young cock picks up a generalized song in his first summer and then develops the finer details by copying his neighbours' during his first breeding season.

The cock courts his mate by sleeking down his feathers to display the white wing patches and raising the wing nearest to the hen to show off his red flank. The hen weaves a neat nest camouflaged with lichen in the fork of a tree. It has been suggested that early Stone Age basket work may have been inspired by the Chaffinch's nest. Only one brood is reared although a pair may make up to six attempts if the first nest fails.

In autumn, the young birds form flocks, and if food becomes really scarce the resident adults may form groups of separate sexes. In winter, our resident population is joined by migrant birds from Scandinavia; the hens moving further south than the cocks. The Swedish scientist Linnaeus noticed that the few birds that remained around his home in winter were males and this suggested to him their scientific name *coelebs* meaning bachelor.

C.F. Tunnicliffe

Greenfinch

In certain areas, Greenfinches (*Carduelis chloris*) are some of the most common bird-table visitors. In hard weather, these birds used to rely on stackyards as their main source of food but agricultural changes have forced them to move into towns and villages when frosts and snow make natural food difficult to find.

During the hard weather of 1963, a study in the Oxford area showed that 97 per cent of the Greenfinch's food consisted of peanuts. In some gardens, over 1 000 different individuals were ringed in one winter. This is an excellent example of a main food source being changed by social experience – one bird learnt from another and the new habit rapidly spread throughout the whole population. In a similar way, Greenfinches first started eating the seeds of *Daphne* in the north of England in the 1930s. By the 1950s the habit had spread throughout Britain and by 1960 it had reached the Continent.

The Greenfinch's choicest habitats are large overgrown gardens and church-yards with thick evergreens and tall hedges. They also breed in young conifer plantations but on farmland they form only 3 per cent of the total bird population.

The large, stout bill of the Greenfinch enables it to tackle really large, hard seeds. Along the edges of woods it takes elm and dog's mercury in summer, rose and bramble in autumn and yew and hornbeam in winter. On wasteland, charlock and redleg form an important part of its diet.

In March, the cock bird begins his monotonous wheezy call to attract his mate. The nest is rather loosely constructed of fine twigs, moss and grass in a thick hedge or on a flat bough. However, unlike most finches the male helps with the work and two broods are usually reared.

By the end of August with the breeding season over, Greenfinches start to congregate in large flocks with other finches to feed and roost. The usual number is between 50 to 300 but in midwinter there may be as many as 2 000 birds at a single roost. Clumps of rhododendrons and other evergreen shrubs are favourite sites and on winter afternoons the aerial displays are fascinating to watch.

These roosts, of course, help to reduce predation, by the very nature of the site and the fact that several hundred pairs of eyes will spot a predator far quicker than one pair. They may also act as information centres – at dawn the unsuccessful individuals follow the successful birds to a more lucrative food source.

Bullfinch

A mixture of admiration and exasperation is the usual reaction if someone has a pair of Bullfinches (*Pyrrhula pyrrhula*) in the garden. You cannot dispute the fact that the male, with his splendid pink breast and grey and black back, is one of our most handsome birds. However, his habit of feeding on buds may only be a nuisance to the gardener but to a commercial fruit-grower it can mean a crop of a few kilograms instead of several tonnes.

The Bullfinch problem is by no means a new one, since as long ago as the Middle Ages the bird had a price on its head. It is interesting to note that over most of Europe and Asia the Bullfinch inhabits northern coniferous forests and it is only at the two extremes of its range, Britain and Japan, where it has moved into deciduous woods and shrubland, that it is a pest species.

It is difficult for the average person to envisage serious Bullfinch damage. A couple of pairs may feed on the buds of a japonica, forsythia, a pear or apple tree, and there is no apparent damage to the resulting crop. In commercial orchards, there may be as many as fifty birds systematically working from the tip of each branch and removing as many as forty-five buds per minute. Each tree may carry no more than 1 000 buds and therefore the damage can be horrifying.

Fruit buds apart, a Bullfinch's choicest meal is seeds. In autumn, it feeds on birch, nettle and bramble seeds, and ash later in the season. If ash seeds are plentiful the Bullfinch will continue to feed on these until the supply is exhausted in about February or March; it then moves on to buds. However, ash trees only have a good crop of seeds every two years, thus every other year the fruit-growers suffer.

In the breeding season, the Bullfinch is nowhere near such a problem. The flocks break up into pairs, which have stayed together throughout the winter, and build their light but strong, platform-like nests in a dense thicket or shrub. The hen, which can be recognized by her duller coloured breast, incubates the eggs. Food for the young is collected in special throat pouches which are only developed in the breeding season. The young are reared on a mixture of seeds (fat hen, dandelion, and sow thistle) small insects and spiders. The percentage of animal matter is slowly reduced and by the time they leave the nests the fledglings are feeding entirely on seeds.

Ringing recoveries have shown that in the first autumn most birds only venture a few miles from their birthplace, and therefore Bullfinches are the most sedentary of all our finches.

Goldfinch

Goldfinches (*Carduelis carduelis*) are now very common in orchards, along roadsides or in a wild part of the garden, but this was not always the case. In the nineteenth century they were much prized as cage birds. At one site in Sussex, about 32 000 were caught each year, but public opinion was aroused and by 1881 the practice had been banned in Britain.

Goldfinches feed almost exclusively on the seeds of the Compositae plant family which includes thistle, dandelion, groundsel, ragwort and burdock. Their fine, sharply pointed bill is used like a pair of tweezers for extracting the seeds which are embedded deeply in the seed heads. The Goldfinch is the only finch that can tackle teasel seeds, and Charles Darwin noticed that more of the males than the females fed on this plant. In fact the cock's slightly longer bill makes him four times as efficient as his mate at extracting these seeds.

The hen Goldfinch builds her nest high up near the end of a branch; garden fruit trees are a favourite spot. The nest of moss and grass is bound to the bough with spider's silk and has a deeper cup than most finch nests to make certain the eggs are safe during high winds.

Carduline finches, the group to which Goldfinches, Greenfinches, Linnets and Siskins belong, nest in loose colonies. The territory defended by each pair is very small, about 240 sq m (285 sq yd) and this boundary is reduced even more once the eggs are laid so that two pairs may well be nesting in the same tree.

This marked difference in territory size compared with that of the Chaffinch (thirty Goldfinches can fit into one Chaffinch territory) is related to their different diet and the way in which this food is distributed. The insects taken by the Chaffinch are fairly evenly dispersed in its habitat therefore, by defending a sizable area, the bird will always find sufficient food to feed its young. However, for the seed-eating Goldfinch the situation is different. Food is found in great abundance, but only for a short time, in localized areas which may be some distance apart. If the Goldfinch defended a feeding territory it might soon find itself with insufficient food. It is therefore better to defend a small nesting area and forage communally.

Our British Goldfinches are partial migrants. A study in Oxford showed that four-fifths of the population moved out during the main autumn migration. They leave Britain via the south-east coast using the shortest sea crossing and winter down the west side of Europe from the Low Countries to Spain. Some British birds also move across to Ireland.

Linnet

The Linnet (*Acanthis cannabina*) is one of our most common finches but very often passes unnoticed. These birds mainly frequent open wastes and commons but they do come into big gardens adjoining open country or large urban parks.

In breeding plumage, the cock Linnet is extremely smart with his greyish head, warm chestnut body and bright crimson forehead and breast – the amount of pink colouring varies considerably between individuals. The hen is duller in colour and her main distinguishing marks are the white edges to the wing and tail feathers.

The stubby bill immediately identifies the Linnet as a seed-eater. However, the beak is slightly smaller than that of the Greenfinch and therefore the bird takes proportionately smaller seeds. On the Continent, as its Latin name suggests, it feeds on hemp. In Britain, the cheerful twittering flocks depend almost entirely on weed seeds from agricultural crops. Charlock and seeds from the cabbage family form a third of its diet and those of redleg, fat hen and chickweed are also taken. For short periods, Linnets feed on dandelions and thistles but, unlike the Goldfinch, they can only take the latter while they are seeding and the fluffy parachute heads can be pulled out with the seeds attached.

Changes in agricultural practice seem to have had little effect on the Linnet population. There are signs of local declines but no apparent general trend. This, therefore, suggests that the Linnets themselves have adapted to the removal of hedges, reclamation of marginal land and the use of herbicides. By contrast, in southern Finland and Sweden, Linnets were widespread on farmland at the beginning of the century, but during the 1930s and 1940s as farming became more mechanized and efficient the birds disappeared. They have now made a comeback as urban birds nesting in small towns, villages, parks and gardens. Perhaps this will happen in Britain in the future.

Linnets are colonial breeders, nesting close to the ground in gorse or bramble bushes. The cocks attract their mates with their sweet musical notes and in Victorian and Edwardian times their persistent twittering made them highly favoured as cage birds.

In winter, most Linnets move across to the European mainland, usually staying around the Bay of Biscay. Those remaining in Britain join up with other finch flocks and feed on wasteland, saltmarshes and coastal mudflats. On the coast, they are often accompanied by their close relative, the Twite, which is sometimes called the mountain linnet since it replaces the Linnet in the uplands of north-west Britain.

Siskin

In most parts of Britain the Siskin (*Carduelis spinus*) is still only a winter visitor from northern Europe. The continental birds arrive in late September to the end of October and greatly outnumber our own small breeding population.

They feed primarily on alder seeds, delicately removing them from the open cones. However, in the mid-1960s, in several areas of southern Britain, they were attracted to fat that was hung out in gardens for tits. They have now become regular winter visitors to gardens taking both peanuts and fat and finding them particularly attractive when they are inside a red or orange plastic-mesh bag.

Breeding Siskins were originally confined to the native Scots pine woods of the Highlands, but with the spread of commercial conifer forests their breeding range expanded. They now nest in spruce plantations in Ireland, East Anglia, Wales, Northumberland, Devon and the New Forest.

During the breeding season the males have a musical flight call which often accompanies their circular display flight. The nest is small and neat, and situated high in a conifer tree. Winter flocks of Siskins use a high pitched contact call as they move through the trees.

Redpoll

From a distance the Redpoll (*Acanthis flammea*) can easily be mistaken for a Linnet. However, it is a smaller, chubbier bird and can be identified by its distinctive metallic call, 'chuch-uch-uch-uch', and bounding flight. In winter, these birds often feed with Siskin flocks high in the branches of riverside alders. They are amazingly agile, hanging upside down, twisting and turning as they feed on the cones.

In the breeding season they are common in the north but, in Ireland and the southern parts of England, they are more local and restricted to the hilly areas. They breed mainly in birch scrub, alder and sallow thickets, but have recently started nesting in young plantations, overgrown hedgerows and even gardens.

Siskins and Redpolls both feed on tree seeds, the abundance of which fluctuates from year to year, whereas other finches feed on the less variable seed crop from herbaceous plants. Their whole ecology enables them to exploit this unpredictable food source most efficiently. The numbers breeding in any area change in relation to their food supply; their migration times and routes are also much more flexible than those of other birds. In years of plenty, they leave the northern breeding areas later in autumn and move less far south, stopping wherever food is abundant. In Britain, therefore, winter numbers are only high when the seed crops have failed in Scandinavia. If there is still plenty of food here in the spring large numbers will stay and breed. Unlike many birds, these small finches show no tendency to return to the area where they were hatched or had previously bred.

C.F. Tunnicliffe

Treecreeper

The subtle brown plumage of the Treecreeper (*Certhia familiaris*) helps it to blend almost invisibly with the bark of a tree. Like the woodpeckers, although not related to them, this bird has specially stiffened tail feathers to give it extra support when climbing. It feeds on insects and their larvae by spiralling up from the base of a tree, and every now and again it jerks sideways to investigate a nook or cranny. It pushes in its scimitar-like bill and delicately picks an edible morsel. Once it reaches the top, it leisurely flies down to the base of the next tree.

Mature woodlands are the Treecreeper's usual home, but it will visit well timbered gardens and can sometimes even be seen searching an old garden wall for insects.

The call and song of the Treecreeper are extremely high pitched and are frequently heard in early spring. The nest is carefully concealed behind a flap of bark or in a crevice of an old tree. When returning to the nest, the Treecreeper flies to the base of the tree and winds its way upwards until suddenly (and it is always the moment when you are not looking) it will vanish without trace into the nest.

Although the Treecreeper is a bird of deciduous woods, surveys by the British Trust for Ornithology have shown that when the population is high after a good breeding year, it will nest in coniferous forests as it always does in Europe. Somewhat surprisingly its breeding success in conifers is higher than in broadleaved woods. One may well ask the question why is the Treecreeper not more abundant in the coniferous woods in Britain? The answer is simple – commercial plantations are devoid of dead or decaying trees with split or peeling bark in which the Treecreeper can nest. This also explains the success of artificial nest-boxes in coniferous forests and their relative failure in broadleaved woods.

In winter, the Treecreeper becomes far more gregarious, roving the woods with parties of tits and Goldcrests. Its favourite roosting sites are Wellingtonias, since the bark is soft enough for the Treecreeper's delicate bill to excavate a hole. Few trees are without these characteristic hollows about 2–5m (6–16ft) above the ground. The roosting bird presses itself against the trunk of the tree and fluffs out its feathers; this camouflages the bird by breaking up the outline of its body and also reduces heat loss.

Nuthatch

You can tell at a glance if a Nuthatch (*Sitta europaea*) has taken over one of your nest-boxes since the bird carefully plasters round the hole until it is exactly the right size. You will also be unable to examine the contents as this security conscious bird meticulously seals the lid and even cements the box to the tree. Natural nest-holes are mudded over in a similar way, and one nest in the fork of an apple tree in Sussex contained over 5lb ($2\frac{1}{4}$kg) of mud.

The Nuthatch is a bird of woods, parkland and large mature gardens. It feeds on beech mast and acorns which it carefully jams into a vice-like crevice in the bark of an old tree before hammering them open to extract the kernel. The hammering can be heard from quite a distance and is a sure sign that there is a Nuthatch in the area.

A few winters ago, a Nuthatch was one of my regular visitors to a spiral pea-nut feeder. It was always a slightly later riser than the Great or Blue Tits but never had to wait its turn – it was definitely the dominant bird. It soon became quite tame and I could stand close to the window watching it hammer the feeder with the whole force of its body. The bird seemed to devour nuts at an incredible speed, but on watching more closely I realized it was simply storing them in a nearby tree.

Nuts are, of course, only seasonal food and at other times of the year the Nuthatch searches the branches of trees for insects and spiders. This bird lacks the specially stiffened tail feathers of the Treecreeper and woodpeckers and scurries up and down the bark of the trees relying only on the strong grip of its claws.

The handsome slate-grey and chestnut plumage may appear slightly garish for the more somber colours of its woodland habitat. However, if you look for a Nuthatch on a grey or lichen-covered tree, only its movements or clear whistle-like call will give it away. In flight it can easily be confused with the Lesser Spotted Woodpecker, but is best told by its paler, uniform grey colouring.

The distribution of the Nuthatch is somewhat patchy even where suitable woods exist. It does not breed in Ireland and is only occasionally recorded in Scotland and northern England. The disappearance of Nuthatches from central London parks and much of northern England in the nineteenth century may have been the result of an increase in atmospheric pollution which reduced its insect food.

Great Spotted Woodpecker

A loud drumming sound is always the first sign that there is a Great Spotted Woodpecker (*Dendrocopos major*) about. You may catch a quick glimpse of a pied body as it switchbacks its way to another tree where once again it becomes hidden from view.

The Great Spotted Woodpecker is at home in both deciduous and coniferous woods and since the 1950s has even moved into suburban parks and gardens. It can be tempted down to a bird-table with nuts and fat provided there are sufficient trees to allow a concealed approach.

The Great Spotted Woodpecker well deserves its reputation as nature's carpenter. Its powerful neck muscles and chisel-like bill are ideally designed for wood boring. Once a grub or insect has been located the woodpecker's long sticky barbed tongue dextrously hooks it out from its deep crevice. The bird is also a most proficient nutcracker, splitting the hardest peach or plum stone by wedging it into a crack. In the breeding season the woodpecker has the unfortunate habit of chipping open nest-boxes occupied by tits in order to feed on the nestlings.

Unlike most birds which sing to advertise their territories, woodpeckers make a drumming sound on a resonant dead branch. The drumming can be heard over half a kilometre (quarter of a mile) away and wards off intruding woodpeckers, but plays no part in courtship.

The female is attracted to the territory by the male's quivering wing display and remains if she approves of his nest-hole; they then complete the nest together. Old dead birch trees are favourite sites and a new chamber is excavated each year. The woodpecker is an untidy worker and fresh wood chips are the telltale signs of a nesting bird.

The Great Spotted Woodpecker has an interesting if not curious distribution. It has never been recorded in Ireland but nested in Scotland until the early part of the nineteenth century and then, according to records, became extinct. Extensive tree felling and competition for nest-holes with Starlings and red squirrels were blamed for the dramatic decline. However, at the beginning of this century the species was once again on the increase, and this has been particularly noticeable recently due to the plentiful supply of insects and suitable nest-sites offered by our dead elms – one of the more fortuitous effects of Dutch elm disease.

Green Woodpecker

The Green Woodpecker (*Picus viridis*) is the largest of the British woodpeckers and, unlike the Great Spotted Woodpecker, it rarely drums. Its shrill, maniacal laughing call has in many counties given rise to the local name, yaffle; while in other areas this species is known as the rainbird, since its call is said to predict rain.

The Green Woodpecker's craving for ants has forced it to abandon a tree-boring, woodland life for a ground-feeding, parkland existence. However, one may well ask what of wood ants which would seem to be the solution to all Green Woodpeckers' problems? Unfortunately, these insects prefer coniferous woodland and are rather local in their distribution. It is the meadow ant, which builds the typical ant hill, that is the Green Woodpecker's main food. In severe winters, it has to pay rather harshly for its conservative tastes since the ant hills are frozen solid or buried deep in the snow and many birds starve to death.

The Green Woodpecker often ventures into large gardens probing the lawns for earthworms and leatherjackets. The long, pale grey droppings, which when broken in half reveal a mass of dark insect exoskeletons, are positive proof that you have had a woodpecker visiting your garden. Green Woodpeckers cannot be easily enticed to the bird-table but in extremely cold, frosty weather I have seen them pecking at windfalls at the far end of a garden.

In the breeding season the Green Woodpecker defends a territory. The yaffle call advertises the boundary limits and if any of its own kind dare to venture across that line the defending bird swings its head from side to side in a snake-like fashion. It also raises its crest and fans out its wings and tail, a warning that is usually quite enough to scare off any rival. In courtship, Green Woodpeckers drop their wings and raise their tails and chase each other spirally round the trunk of a tree.

The Green Woodpecker, like the Great Spotted Woodpecker, is not found in Ireland. It has only recently spread into Scotland, where it is found in the south-west, the central Lowlands and sparsely along the east coast. This increase may be associated with the maturing of forestry plantations where wood ants thrive. By contrast, in the Midlands and north-east England, numbers have failed to recover after the hard winter of 1962–63. This may be associated with the decline in sheep farming and also in rabbit populations (reduced by myxomatosis), as both these species produce short turf where ants abound.

Starling

There is no need to attract Starlings (*Sturnus vulgaris*) to your bird-table. They can be guaranteed to find any convenient food source. These birds are some of the most successful in the world, and the secret of their success is that they have learnt to take advantage of every opportunity that is offered by both man and nature.

This gangster of the bird-table world is extraordinarily catholic in its taste for food – insects, scraps, fruit and seeds – almost anything is eaten. When ants are swarming on summer evenings, Starlings appear as if from nowhere. They feed alongside grazing cattle waiting for disturbed insects and even perch on the backs of sheep to peck out the ticks.

The Starling can be credited with neither grace nor style; it has a stumpy tail, and moves with a jerky walk or bustling run. However, its plumage is its saving grace; on close inspection the dark feathers are shot with iridescent purples and greens and in winter it is star-spangled with white.

Although the Starling's usual song is a mixture of churring whistles and clicks, one of the bird's more curious talents is its mastery of mimicry. In Cumbria I have often been tricked by a Starling imitating a Lapwing; they have been known to mimic telephone bells.

Starlings nest in every kind of habitat except for the most exposed uplands. They prefer a natural nest-hole and will usurp a woodpecker immediately it has finished chipping out a suitable hole. They also take over Sand Martins' holes and even Swifts' nests.

On winter evenings, Starlings congregate in vast flocks of sometimes over a million birds. They are fascinating to watch as they fly into their roost like a never-ending black cloud, twisting and turning in unison. In some country areas their droppings defoliate and even kill trees. However, it is in our cities that they cause the most serious problem. The Department of the Environment and various local authorities wage a continuous battle against the Starling. Various scaring methods have been tried from stuffed owls and rubber snakes to fireworks and recordings of distress calls. Sometimes these methods are successful and the Starlings change their roosts and become someone else's problem.

Blackbird

A cat in the garden and the loud 'tchook, tchook, tchook' alarm call of the Blackbird (*Turdus merula*) warns every other bird of the predator's whereabouts. The Blackbird's song is not in the least raucous; on a spring evening after a shower of rain its rich, mellow warble can equal that of a Nightingale.

The Blackbird was originally a woodland species but over the last 150 years it has been quick to adapt. As the woods were felled it moved first into farmland hedges, later to gardens and parks and even into the centres of towns and cities. City-dwelling Blackbirds find much of their food on bird-tables, and television aerials replace trees as song-posts. Population studies show that the breeding success of Blackbirds is higher on farmland and in suburban gardens than in woodland.

Another secret of the Blackbird's success is its wide and varied diet. Apart from the usual earthworms, insects, spiders, and nuts and berries in winter, they have been known to take lizards, newts, shrews and even trout fry.

Look out of your window on to the grass on any damp, dewy morning and you are likely to see a Blackbird worming. Many people believe that as the bird cocks its head sideways it is listening for a likely meal but this is not true. A blackbird's eyes, unlike ours, are situated at the side of its head and its visual field is therefore at right angles to ours. Furthermore, a bird's eye cannot move in its socket and thus it must cock its head to search the ground near its feet.

The handsome, matt black cock bird with his yellow-orange bill is unmistakeable. The mottled brown hen and the slightly lighter brown juveniles are sometimes confused with Song Thrushes. The Blackbird is very prone to plumage abnormalities and partially albino birds with patches of white feathers are fairly common. Totally albino birds are sometimes reported and leucistic birds, in which the dark pigment is diluted so that they appear paler in colour, also occasionally occur. Total albinism is genetic but both partial albinism and leucism can be induced experimentally by changing the diet. Both the last mentioned conditions occur most widely in urban birds feeding on a high proportion of artificial foods and are probably caused by deficiencies in their diet.

In spring, gatherings of cock Blackbirds parade around with lowered tails and outstretched wings. Once a mate has been chosen pairs will nest in close proximity to one another if food is plentiful. Hedges and small trees are favoured, but Blackbirds use a great variety of sites including potting-sheds and garden machinery. Two or three broods are usually reared, but five successfully raised clutches have been recorded.

Song Thrush

The Song Thrush (*Turdus philomelos*) certainly lives up to its name. Its sweet clear song has made it the poets' favourite bird. Robert Browning's line, 'That's the wise thrush; he sings each song twice over', is most apt as each phrase is repeated twice if not three times.

The Song Thrush nests and feeds in gardens, orchards and in almost every type of woodland. Its habitat choice is remarkably similar to that of the Blackbird. However, it is always outnumbered by the latter. As a rough generalization, the richer and more varied the habitat, the more Song Thrushes it is likely to hold and the more narrowly will the Blackbirds outnumber them.

The islands of the Outer Hebrides and Skye are occupied by a separate darker race of Song Thrush. These birds live on the moors, in the peat hags and are even found along the coast and presumably replace the Ring Ouzel, the Blackbird's counterpart in the uplands.

The Song Thrush is unique among garden birds in its feeding habits for it is a tool-using bird; it opens snails by smashing their shells on an anvil-stone. A large stone sprinkled with a few shattered remains of snail shells may well encourage Song Thrushes to use the anvil in a garden.

The Blackbird lacks this ability but makes up for it in ingenuity. A study showed that a Blackbird could learn to recognize the Song Thrush's hammering sound. The bird would skulk nearby and once the noise had stopped it would dash out and seize the opened snail. This is an excellent example of adaptable behaviour being superior to specialization.

The Song Thrush is a most desirable garden resident, not only as a collector of snails, earwigs, centipedes and spiders but, rather surprisingly for a bird of its size, as an aphid-eater.

The nest is a very solid construction with a hard basin-like mud lining. It is built by the hen alone, usually low in a bush or hedge. Once the young have fledged they move into surrounding cover where they remain, silent and unseen, for several days. However, do not try to rescue the fledglings for they have not been abandoned and are being regularly fed by the parents. If the brood is scattered this can cause disaster as a lost youngster becomes vocal and conspicuous to predators. Be patient, and when the young are a bit older you will soon see the whole family feeding on the grass.

C. F. Tunnicliffe

Mistle Thrush

The country name stormcock is far more descriptive than the more common name Mistle Thrush (*Turdus viscivorus*) since, throughout the year, this bird's loud ringing song is said to forecast rain and stormy weather. The Mistle Thrush may not be the most melodious of thrushes but it is certainly the loudest.

A bird of open country or large gardens, from time immemorial the Mistle Thrush has lived close to man but has remained totally untamed and disdains all artificial feeding and nesting aids.

One of the best places to see Mistle Thrushes is on local playing fields where they busily seek worms and other invertebrate prey. Standing proud and erect they often remain immobile for considerable lengths of time. Unlike our other native thrushes the stormcock is fearless and ventures far from cover. Its song-post is on a high exposed branch in a tree. Its flight is strong and direct showing off the striking white underwing which distinguishes it from the Song Thrush, as does its pale grey coloration and larger size.

In a survey of the fruit-eating habits of the British thrushes, despite its name, there was no record of a Mistle Thrush eating mistletoe berries; in fact it showed a marked preference for yew or holly. It was suggested that the name came from the bird's habit of feeding on the red berries of another species of mistletoe common in the Mediterranean olive groves.

The nest is built in early spring in the fork of a tree. The hen chooses the site and often squats in various likely spots before she selects the final position. The nest is large and untidy with a mud core and lining of grasses, hair and roots. Breeding birds are bold and fearless and defend their nest with astonishing ferocity. They will attack and drive away crows, owls and cats.

As soon as the young have fledged the whole family adopt a nomadic life-style and move away from the breeding ground. It is vitally important for young Mistle Thrushes to remain in contact with their parents and, unlike young Song Thrushes or Blackbirds, they are extremely noisy and easy to spot.

In the 1800s the Mistle Thrush was confined to southern England and Wales but it is now found throughout mainland Britain and Ireland. The reasons for this expansion are obscure; the increase in commercial plantations could be one explanation but it is by no means the only one.

C. F. Tunnicliffe

Fieldfare

When huge groups of the large, slate-headed Fieldfares (*Turdus pilaris*) start to plunder our hawthorn bushes it is a sure sign that winter is here. In the north of England they are called snow birds since often their arrival heralds the snow. They are tough, harsh-voiced birds with striking plumage.

When they first arrive from the north they feed in the roadside hedges on hips and haws. Once this supply is exhausted they move on to nearby fields and meadows to scavenge for slugs, worms and insects.

You rarely see one Fieldfare feeding on its own. Flocks of up to 200 birds are usual and they are often accompanied by just as many hangers-on in the form of Redwings, Starlings and others. They form a well disciplined group sprinkled thinly over the ground with all birds facing the same direction and each individual about 1m (3ft) from the next. They walk in short spurts, stopping to have a quick look round for danger. As the day draws in they move en masse to their regular roosts which are usually on the ground among coarse herbage, hedges or shrubberies.

Fieldfares are nomadic throughout the winter moving around to wherever food is abundant; in severe conditions they will even feed in town parks on the berries of ornamental shrubs. A few windfalls scattered on a rough piece of ground at the bottom of a large garden may well attract them.

In April and early May Fieldfares form much larger flocks. In the Eden valley in Cumbria, I have seen several thousand birds stretching for field upon field. Most eventually move north to their Scandinavian breeding grounds where they nest communally, often up to five in one tree, in birch woods, parks and town gardens.

Since 1967, a handful have remained in Britain, nesting on the moors, wooded hill slopes or even farmlands of Scotland and northern England. Like the Mistle Thrush, they fiercely defend their nest-sites from all predators.

Over the past century, the Fieldfare has slowly extended its breeding range westwards. This may be due to climatic changes causing colder springs. In Britain, this bird is afforded special protection under Schedule I of the Protection of Birds Acts, which means wilful disturbance of a bird at its nest can incur a penalty of up to £500.

Redwing

On late October or early November afternoons when out walking the dog, I always listen for the plaintive, far-carrying calls of migrating Redwings (*Turdus iliacus*). You may not be able to see the birds high overhead but, if you hear them one night, the following morning you will probably see a few small parties of stragglers passing overhead or feeding in the fields and hedges.

Redwings are small, delicate thrushes with red flanks and give the impression of being totally unsuited to the harsh northern life. They are some of the first casualties if the weather is severe and often move into suburban gardens after a hard frost or a fall of snow. However, if possible, they shun human habitation and prefer to join the Fieldfare flocks feeding on berries in the hedges.

Redwings show a greater liking for tall bushes and shrubs than Fieldfares and are less likely to venture far from cover. They are more fussy in their choice of feeding grounds preferring good quality grassland which is no doubt related to their diet. This consists of mainly insects, worms, slugs, snails and other small invertebrates. They take little vegetable matter apart from gorging themselves on berries when they first arrive. Wet meadows provide highly suitable feeding grounds, and I have watched a Redwing busily searching under leaves for insects at the side of a village green.

Redwings prefer to roost in thick warm cover – hawthorn, laurel or rhododendron bushes are ideal. Ringing has shown that these birds are by no means consistent in their choice of wintering resort, since an individual ringed in Britain was recorded the following winter in Cyprus. Flocks in England move across to Ireland to avoid hard weather and return when conditions improve.

The Redwing is slowly extending its breeding range and has regularly nested in Scotland for the last decade; in 1972 the Scottish population was estimated at around 300 pairs. They are very variable in their choice of nest-sites selecting birch, pine and oak woods, or even large gardens, preferably close to running water.

Its song is very distinctive and consists of about five descending fluted notes delivered from a high perch in a tree. The low nest is typical of a thrush with an inner mud-cup, lined with grass. The Redwing, like the Fieldfare, is a specially protected species.

Waxwing

The Waxwing (*Bombycilla garrulus*) is a curious looking bird but nonetheless beautiful. It is hardly surprising that when Waxwings appear, often in large numbers, they arouse the interest of both the birdwatcher and the man in the street.

The Waxwing is about the size of a Starling, and one of the most striking features of its plumage are the red 'wax-tips' to some of the secondary wing feathers from which the bird takes its name. These are in fact modified ends of the feather shaft.

Waxwings nest in the subarctic birch or pine forests of Scandinavia and the Russian taiga, building a nest of lichen and twigs. In most years, the majority of the population winters close to its breeding grounds, while a few migrate to central Europe. However, every few years, and sometimes for several years in succession, they move out en masse to winter throughout Europe; this is known as irruptive behaviour.

The breeding and wintering movements of Waxwings are still not well understood. The reasons for such invasions are thought to be a combination of lack of rowan berries and high numbers of birds. Rowan berries are the Waxwings' chief winter food and can vary widely in abundance from year to year, a heavy crop very often being followed by a light one. A good berry harvest results from warm weather in the spring when the trees are in flower, and thus a good breeding season may be followed by a plentiful supply of winter food. The following year berries may be scarce but the Waxwing numbers will still be high, and so the birds must move out to find sufficient winter food.

The first Waxwing winter recorded in Britain was as long ago as 1697–98, and one of the largest recent irruptions was in 1965–66 when more than 11 000 birds were recorded here in two weeks in November.

On arrival, the Waxwings first feed on rowan berries but when these are finished they turn to pyracantha and cotoneaster. They are extremely tame and can be watched at very close range; in Norfolk an observed bird ate 390 berries in two and a half hours. Later in the winter, they even come to bird-tables where they feed on seeds, bread and apples. They have also been recorded eating crab apples; the birds started at the top of the tree and slowly worked their way down. However, once on the ground they often fell victim to cats, not only because of their inherent tameness, but also because many of them were intoxicated after eating the fermenting fruit.

In spring, after these large invasions, displaying birds have been seen in suitable nesting habitats in Scotland. However, as yet, there has been no definite confirmation of breeding.

Whitethroat

Like all members of the warbler family, the Whitethroat (*Sylvia communis*) is a summer visitor arriving in mid-April and occasionally staying as late as October. Usually the first sign that the Whitethroat has returned is its bright, chattering song. Search among hawthorn, thick brambles or clumps of nettles and you may spot the bird or, if you are lucky, you may see a male bird performing his tumbling display flight.

The Whitethroat is a bird of shrubland and with the Enclosure Act of the eighteenth century even more suitable habitats became available. To encourage Whitethroats into your garden, order and tidiness must be kept to a minimum. The thicker the undergrowth and the wilder the vegetation the better.

Until recently, the Whitethroat was one of our commonest migrants but in 1969 its population crashed sensationally to less than a quarter of its former level. The British Trust for Ornithology's Common Bird Census enabled us to detect this change and it was confirmed by ringing data. This showed that in 1968, 10 205 adult birds had been trapped and ringed, but this total had fallen to 1 797 in the following year. Ups and downs in migrant bird populations have always occurred; 200 years ago Gilbert White recorded a drop in numbers, but it is only now that we have an explanation.

There were two possible reasons: first, the Whitethroat had suffered serious losses on its journey to and from Britain; or secondly, conditions had been unfavourable in its West African winter quarters. Checks with meteorological records proved that on most days during the actual migration the weather conditions had been perfect, which ruled out the first possibility. Scientists then looked at conditions in the Whitethroat's wintering area, the semi-arid steppe country bordering the southern edge of the Sahara-Sahel zone. In the 1950s, the rainfall there had been above average and the nomadic tribes had moved in to graze their cattle. In 1968, the rains failed and there has been little since. Compared with the previous period of drought the area was vastly over-populated with people and animals. A famine situation was created, over three-and-a-half million cattle died, millions of tonnes of grain were lost and six million people faced starvation. There was little hope for the Whitethroats since all the berry-bearing shrubs on which they fed disappeared without trace.

There is now nothing left for the Whitethroats in the Sahel. It would be better for the birds to winter further south, but evolutionary changes such as these take time. We must wait and see how well the species will overcome this drastic reduction in numbers.

Swallow

The sound of the Cuckoo and the sight of the Swallow (*Hirundo rustica*) herald the spring. The Swallows' return in early April is always a cheerful occasion, their faithfulness to their old nest-sites and their association with man's buildings have won them a special place in man's affection since Greek and Roman times.

For the first few days (or even weeks) after their arrival they stay around water meadows, marshes and sewage farms where insect life is plentiful. Their short bills surrounded with bristles funnel insects into their wide gapes like aerial nets. All day they hunt for flies and at dusk they roost gregariously in the reeds. Once the weather improves and insects are plentiful elsewhere they move out to their traditional sites.

True natural breeding sites are very rare, although Swallows are still recorded nesting on seacliffs and in caves in mountainous regions. In wild open country the Swallow will even build its nest on the side of large raptor nests. Old barns and cowsheds are now most favoured as the Swallow does not have to venture far in search of food. If you have Swallows nesting nearby, open a garage or shed and you may well encourage a pair to move in. Although the adults return to their old sites, last year's young will be looking for a suitable spot in the neighbourhood.

The nest is made of pellets of mud mixed with saliva and fibrous material. It is usually supported by a beam, the top of an inner wall or a single nail or peg and lined with hair and feathers. To collect mud for their nests these aerial acrobats must land, and you only have to watch them to realize how out of place they are on the ground. Their short legs are totally unsuitable for walking. If there is a drought a bucket of water tipped in a dusty corner will provide local Swallows with a convenient source of building material.

Four to five eggs are laid and the young are fed on bundles of insects delivered to each individual in turn. The nest is often used twice and once the final brood has fledged the birds will still roost there. In early autumn, they return to their communal roosts in the reed beds. This led Aristotle to suppose that Swallows overwintered under the mud in a comatose state, emerging when warmed by the spring sun. Even Gilbert White was uncertain of the facts and believed that, as he saw an occasional bird in November and December, they must all winter in holes in seacliffs. However, these were probably young from a third brood which sometimes do not attempt to migrate. By October the majority of birds have stored up sufficient fat reserves to make the flight to their South African wintering resort.

House Martin

The House Martin (*Delichon urbica*) is one of the few birds that has benefited from the spread of man's concrete jungle. Nesting on the outer walls of buildings, under eaves or buttresses, 'the temple-haunting martlet's' association with man was well known in Shakespeare's time. Surveys in London showed that there has been a steady spread and growth of colonies in the inner city related to the introduction of the Clean Air Act in 1954 which has made 'aerial plankton' far more plentiful. However, the House Martin has by no means abandoned its more primitive haunts; cliff-nesting colonies can still be found all round our coast, particularly in the east of Scotland.

Unlike the Swallow, the House Martin is far more communal, found in small colonies of three or four nests, or in groups of as many as forty in farm yards and under bridges. House Martins are less traditional about their nest-sites and sometimes move to a different area to rear their second brood.

Martins are far less quarrelsome than most colonial nesters. The mud nests butt up to one another and it is not uncommon for pairs to become slightly confused over ownership and share the feeding of the same brood. However, one feud which constantly exists is that between House Martins and House Sparrows. Whenever possible the sparrows will evict a pair of martins from their partly built nest and have even been known to tear holes in the side to eject the eggs or young.

Watching these graceful birds you would never guess that they are plagued by a multitude of parasites. A single nest was found to contain 452 fleas, flat-flies, bugs and mites. In addition to the nest parasites, the birds themselves suffer from at least three species of lice and four species of mites.

House Martins arrive in this country about a week or ten days later than Swallows. As they hawk the sky for insects they are easily distinguished from the latter by their black and white appearance. The adult Swallows also have long tail-streamers, but in the autumn, this is not a reliable characteristic since their young have short tails.

After rearing two or even three broods, House Martins gather in flocks along telegraph wires or trees often in the company of Swallows. In October they depart for Africa, their destination still being something of a mystery.

Pied Wagtail

The Pied Wagtail (*Motacilla alba*) is equivalent to a walking House Martin, for it lives on flying insects which it pursues on foot making only short sallies into the air. It lives in close association with man but has never lost its nervousness or mistrust of him. By contrast, it shows no fear of cattle and will feed between their feet; it will even perch on the backs of sheep, flitting into the air to catch a passing fly.

Presumably in days gone by, the Pied Wagtail nested only in the banks of rivers and streams but nowadays, apart from the densest of woods and the highest moors, it breeds almost everywhere in Britain. It has moved into city centres and despite its colloquial name of water wagtail is not so tied to the waterside as the Grey Wagtail.

The Pied Wagtail spends most of its waking hours running swiftly here and there in search of insects, over a lawn, around a farmyard or along the water's edge, constantly jerking its long tail up and down. The reason for the incessant tail movement is not known but it does not appear to play any part in display. However, several other unrelated waterside birds, such as the Dipper and Common Sandpiper, bob up and down continuously, so possibly this may help camouflage the birds against a background of constantly moving water.

The black back of the cock distinguishes it from the hen which is more grey and white in colour. During the breeding season the pairs are well spaced out since the cocks are extremely aggressive; they will attack their own reflection in windows and car hub-caps or wing-mirrors. Rival males face each other in a jerky dancing flight with much warbling, twittering and repeating of the usual 'chizzick' call-note.

The nest is in any kind of hole; around buildings it may be on a ledge or in a crack in a stone wall. In the garden, the birds use open-fronted nest-boxes but if you are building a new stone wall do not be overzealous with your pointing. A small crack will provide an ideal home for a wagtail.

Although some Pied Wagtails fly southwards to winter in warmer climates, many remain in Britain feeding in parties during the day and roosting in large numbers. They like to be warm at night and in some areas they gather in greenhouses and have become a horticultural pest. They also roost in buildings, or on roofs and trees in town centres, and in one place the floodlit shrubs round a motorway transport café were selected. More natural sites are reedbeds which, in autumn, are often shared with migrating Swallows.

Grey Wagtail

The sombre title Grey Wagtail (*Motacilla cinerea*) is most inappropriate for this graceful yellow and grey bird and leads to many being misidentified as Yellow Wagtails. The Grey has a slimmer build than the Pied but the juveniles of the two species can easily be confused; however, young Greys always show some yellow coloration on their underparts.

Grey Wagtails are not common garden birds unless you happen to have a fast flowing stream at the bottom of your garden. These birds are mainly found near upland streams but, over the last thirty years, their breeding range has extended southwards. They now nest near weirs and mill-races in locks on canals and near outflows of lakes and reservoirs.

I have spent many a happy hour watching Grey Wagtails on a shallow, babbling stream in Cumbria. They flit up and down from stone to stone, darting sideways or upwards to snatch a mayfly, or walk sedately with head and neck dipping forward at every step, picking small snails from among the boulders.

In early spring, pairs perform a beautiful display flight spreading and raising their long, slim tails while they utter a soft, plaintive note. The Grey Wagtail's normal call is a shrill, high-pitched 'tzitzi' similar to that of the Pied Wagtail.

The nest is mainly built by the hen under the roots of a riverside tree or in a small crevice under a bridge. The same site is often used for several years but it is not known if the same pair returns each year. If there are a number of similar ledges, such as on a bridge girder, a pair of Grey Wagtails will often start to build several nests as they are apparently incapable of recognizing an individual site.

As winter draws in, the Grey Wagtails that have bred in the northern regions of Britain move southwards to lowland streams, cress-beds and sewage farms. During the day they feed singly but at dusk they move into communal roosts in reedbeds, or in trees or hedges near water.

Grey Wagtail populations are severely hit when rivers and streams freeze over and food becomes unobtainable. It is at times like these that they may be seen in towns or down by the coast. The hard winters of 1961–2 and 1963–4 caused a drastic reduction in numbers but the population appears to be able to recover quite quickly.

Kingfisher

Walking along a stream one may hear a shrill piping call, there is a flash of iridescent blue and the Kingfisher (*Alcedo atthis*) has gone. Despite its brilliant plumage, more akin to a bird of the tropics, it is easy to miss even a brief glimpse of the Kingfisher, since its habit of flying straight and close to the water helps to blend it surprisingly well with the background.

In the past, the Kingfisher's life was one of human persecution. In Victorian times, for example, these birds were in great demand as stuffed ornaments and their feathers were used to decorate ladies' hats. They were caught in specially designed Kingfisher nets hung across streams.

In 1954, prospects improved when the bird was afforded special protection under the Protection of Birds Acts. However, another threat, pollution, had already appeared on the scene. Sewage effluent kills the small fry on which the Kingfisher feeds. Persistent chemicals used in agriculture run off into the streams and are taken up by the Kingfisher's prey. These toxins gradually accumulate in the bird's body causing breeding failure or death. Further dangers to this splendid bird are nylon fishing lines; when carelessly thrown away they can become a lethal trap for many riverside birds.

The Kingfisher catches its prey of bullheads and sticklebacks by diving from a branch like an arrow (the whole process takes only a fraction of a second), or it may sometimes hover over the water like a miniature Osprey before plunging in to catch its victim. The fish is then beaten to death on a stone; you can recognize a Kingfisher's 'execution block' by its glistening cover of fish scales. Food is impossible to obtain when the Kingfisher's home stream freezes over and the birds must move downstream towards the sea. In such conditions they have even been known to take suet from bird-tables.

Each pair of Kingfishers has its own stretch of river which the birds regularly patrol like well-drilled soldiers. The excavation of the nest-hole, which can stretch as far as 1m (3ft) into the bank, may take several weeks. To start it off, the birds must hurl themselves at the bank driving their bills into the soil. Once an edge has been made, work becomes slightly easier and one bird mounts guard while the other digs. The eggs are laid on a mound of bones and excreta, and by the time the young leave the nest, conditions have become most insanitary. Many young die during their first months of life due to starvation or drowning, for although the basic feeding technique is instinctive only practice makes perfect.

Jay

The Jay (*Garrulus glandarius*) is the most gaily adorned of our British crows but, rather disappointingly, it is also the most elusive. The loud, resonant 'kraah' and a fleeting glimpse of a white rump as the bird disappears into the next thicket is often all you see. Jays are sly, mistrustful birds and with good reason; they are the bane of every gamekeeper's or fruit-grower's life. In certain areas where persecution has decreased, they have become far more confiding and can even be tempted to the bird-table to take fruit or left-over vegetables. The Jay can very quickly dispose of large amounts of food by packing it neatly away in its special throat pouch. Once back in the wood it stores the food in any likely hole.

In autumn, Jays gather large quantities of acorns which they bury for the winter. The oak forests which spread over much of Britain may well owe their wide distribution to the Jays' absent-mindedness. However, these birds show a remarkable memory for most of their buried treasure. A hungry Jay flies straight to a food cache and, without even a search, digs up its meal. If a Woodpigeon unwittingly ventures too close, the Jay will drive it off and often goes to the trouble of removing the acorn and burying it elsewhere.

In spring, Jays form large noisy gatherings. The birds chase through the woods in a follow-my-leader fashion. In an open clearing they face each other with raised crests and fluffed out feathers, unfolding their wings to reveal their beautiful, pale blue patches. This behaviour probably helps in pair formation since mated birds rarely take part in such antics.

Like the Starling, the Jay is an excellent mimic but it only imitates the alarm calls of other species. For example, when disturbed at a night roost, Jays often hoot like an owl. It has been suggested that this mimicry is used to convey detailed information as to the nature of the danger to the other roosting birds. Apart from man, the Jay has few predators; however, Tawny Owls will take roosting birds or hens on the nest.

A Jay's nest is always well hidden, usually fairly low in the tops of shrubs or the fork of a tree, but only a few minutes flight from the nearest oak. The nest is built by both sexes; the hen incubates the eggs and is brought food by the cock. The young are fed on insects and caterpillars and it is while the pair are rearing young that they prey on other birds' nestlings.

Magpie

Bold and elegant in its black and white suiting, the Magpie (*Pica pica*) has been credited with the power to foretell good and evil.

A recent survey carried out by the Young Ornithologists' Club, on the numbers of Magpies visiting gardens, showed that these birds are definitely becoming more common in town gardens. They are now nesting in the London parks and a few years ago I found a nest in a large garden in the centre of Birmingham.

Some interesting facts about the Magpie's diet also came to light. Many young members thought that nesting songbirds attracted Magpies to their gardens. These birds were reported coming to bird-tables to feed on fat, bread, nuts and kitchen scraps. They stole chicken and rabbit food and one Magpie pinched dog biscuits from one house and dunked them in the next-door pond. Spiders and insects are the natural food of Magpies, except in winter when they take grain, berries and vegetables and may often be seen scavenging on road-side casualties. In one Sussex garden that I knew, a Magpie became addicted to slow-worms and lizards and almost succeeded in annihilating the total population.

There are many tales of Magpies stealing shiny objects. This mainly occurs in captive or tame birds which are being regularly supplied with food. Due to their inquisitiveness (and perhaps boredom) they show great interest in every object whether edible or inedible.

Magpies have a rather fascinating form of feather care (also seen in many other passerine birds) known as anting. The bird delicately holds an ant in the tip of its bill in such a way that the body fluids are squirted onto the feathers like a living aerosol spray. There has been much dispute over the purpose of anting but it seems likely that the formic acid from the ant helps to rid the bird of fleas and feather lice.

In late winter and early spring, Magpies form ceremonial gatherings of as many as 200 birds. One function of this is thought to be that unpaired birds are able to meet a potential mate; if one member of a pair is killed a gathering of birds will soon follow so that the bereaved individual can select a new partner. In winter, Magpies also congregate in large groups prior to roosting.

The Magpie's nest can be built high in a tree or low in a bush. It is a robust construction with a mud-bowl lined with rootlets and covered with a canopy of prickly sticks. During incubation it is sometimes possible to tell the male from the female, since the hen's tail may be slightly twisted due to her long vigil on the eggs.

Tawny Owl

The Tawny Owl (*Strix aluco*), Britain's most common bird of prey, is more often heard than seen. Stand in any wood, suburban garden or even some of the London parks on a still autumn or spring evening and you will hear its characteristic hoot. The 'towit, towoo' so often used to describe the owl's call is in fact made up of two calls, the sharp 'kerwic', usually uttered by the female, and the answering 'to-woo' of the male.

The Tawny Owl is found throughout Britain wherever there are suitable woods for nesting. However, it has never been recorded in Ireland where its niche is filled by the Long-eared Owl.

Apart from a glimpse in the car head-lights of a shape silently moving through the trees, the Tawny Owl is seldom seen. However, the alarm calls of mobbing tits, Wrens and Blackbirds often disclose the owl's whereabouts. Other clues to its daytime hideaway are creamy dropping at the base of a tree, which is very often a conifer.

Owls, like many other birds, cough up all indigestible parts of their food as pellets. By carefully dissecting these pellets a great deal can be discovered not only about the Tawny Owl's diet but also of the small mammal population of the area. Studies have shown that the owls in central London take mainly birds, such as sparrows, Starlings, Blackbirds and pigeons; the further out of London the Tawny Owl's territory, the larger the proportion of mammals it takes. In deciduous woods, the Tawny Owl feeds largely on bank voles and wood mice. In summer, it also takes beetles and earthworms, while more unusual foods include toads and fish which the owl snatches from the water surface.

Tawny Owls are early breeders and eggs have been found in January. However, the nest, situated in a hole in a tree, is usually occupied by March. These birds are able to adjust their breeding behaviour to the availability of their food supply and in a year when small mammals are scarce few owls will attempt to breed. However, even in a good year, only about half the total population will produce young.

The owlets leave the nest about four weeks after hatching, and are still barely able to fly. They hop and climb around the branches and rely on their parents for food until some time in August. Kind-hearted people are often tempted to rescue these seemingly helpless youngsters. However, do not be misled since the parents will return and are far better at feeding them than any human counterpart. Also, these exceedingly lazy balls of fluff will only learn to hunt if they remain with the adults.

Many owlets die in their first autumn, but once they have established their own territory they are unlikely to move or alter its boundary during their lifetime.

Barn Owl

The history of the Barn Owl (*Tyto alba*) in Britain may go back as far as the Lower Pleistocene (5–600 000 years ago) since a fossil of a Barn Owl-like bird was found in deposits from this era in Norfolk. It is one of the few species of birds which has a worldwide distribution, being found in every continent except the Antarctic.

Its name suggests a close association with man and, feeding mainly on rodents, it should be the farmers' best friend. There have been schemes in this country to encourage the building of nest-boxes in barns. In the Netherlands, some of the farmhouses have large decorative owl boards under the gables with a round opening in the centre so that the birds can gain easy access to the loft.

Barn Owls are reputed to be sedentary but in severe weather they will travel far afield, and in certain years the darker continental form has been recorded in Britain. By comparison 'tawnies' remain in their territories when food is short as they are more likely to find prey in a familiar area.

The Barn Owl is less nocturnal than the Tawny Owl and is often seen quartering a meadow on a winter's afternoon. It hunts mice and voles on the wing (the Tawny Owl simply drops from a branch) and detects prey by both sight and sound. It is therefore essential that all its movements are silent; to aid this the wing feathers are fringed and covered with a velvety pile which cuts down noise in flight. Its large, human-like head with huge eyes facing forwards are all adaptations to nocturnal hunting. The sensitive eyes spaced well apart collect the maximum light available and give the bird binocular vision so that it can judge distances far more efficiently than a bird with eyes at the side of its head. Its hearing is also extremely acute and the widely separated ears help to pinpoint the slightest sound. With a visual acuity between thirty-five and a hundred times our own there is seldom insufficient light for a Barn Owl to see its prey. However, even in total darkness it can catch a mouse by sound alone.

Barn Owls prefer to hunt in open country and the rough grass along road-side verges is ideal for food but is none too safe for the birds, which are frequent road casualties. As if this were not enough, human disturbance, loss of habitat and persistent chemicals have all helped to reduce the population. A survey in England and Wales in 1932, prompted by signs of a decline, indicated that there were about 12 000 pairs. The current total is estimated as between 4 500–9 000 pairs. This decline was the reason for its inclusion among the specially protected species under the Protection of Birds Acts.

House Sparrow

Everyone must know the House Sparrow (*Passer domesticus*) by name but few ever give it a second glance. Familiarity breeds contempt and no bird can more aptly be called man's familiar than the sparrow nesting in our houses and eating food provided directly or indirectly by man. Most people also find sparrows contemptible: the householder dislikes the mess and noise they make under the eaves where they build their untidy, domed nests; the gardener is annoyed by them shedding crocus flowers or uprooting his peas; the farmer finds them a pest for they pinch grain from the standing corn or from the granary; and even birdwatchers seldom have a good word for sparrows since they drive the Robin from the bird-table and evict House Martins from their nests.

However, one cannot help but admire their success which is so closely tied to our own. Sparrows are thought to have spread across Europe from Africa in the wake of Neolithic man, and colonies associated with an isolated farm or on an island only survive as long as man is there to provide their daily bread. Moreover, this ability to exploit our bounty allows them to have up to four broods a season and breed almost all the year round.

Inspite of their dependence on us, sparrows remain wary of people and seldom become really tame. Perhaps they realize the benefits of the association are one sided.

Reed Bunting

The Reed Bunting's name does not suggest a bird one would expect to see in the garden but this species steadily increased as a visitor to the bird-table in the last decade. The British Trust for Ornithology's survey of birds feeding at bird-tables in recent winters showed that Reed Buntings (*Emberiza schoeniclus*) occurred at up to 14 per cent of the sites examined.

They are naturally wetland birds found along the edges of rivers and lakes, in areas of marshy scrub and in wet fields full of rushes. In the early 1960s, at about the time that they began to appear in gardens in winter, they were also found breeding more in dry areas such as hedges in farmland and young plantations, which are habitats more typical of their relative, the Yellow-hammer. This change in habits was first noticed in Kent, and has now been recorded in many other parts of the country.

In winter, the Reed Bunting is a rather inconspicuous sparrow-like bird, which might easily be overlooked. However, during the spring, the males are obviously resplendent in their breeding plumage – a glossy black head and bib, white nape and streaky russet back – declaring their ownership of a patch of undergrowth from the highest reed or stem. Meanwhile, the dowdy hen sits on the nest, well concealed, low in a clump of reeds or sedges.

Willow Warbler and Chiffchaff

The best way to identify most of the warblers is by their song. In the case of the Willow Warbler (*Phylloscopus trochilus*) and the Chiffchaff (*Phylloscopus collybita*)it is the only reliable distinguishing feature for they are both small, agile, greeny-brown birds with paler breasts and bellies. However, Chiffchaffs usually have very dark legs whereas those of most Willow Warblers are pale. Even the most unmusical can recognize the Chiffchaff's song for the bird repeats its name. The Willow Warbler's song is a more musical trill of descending notes.

The Chiffchaff is one of our first summer visitors to arrive in late March and can often be heard singing in parks and town gardens while it is still on passage to its breeding grounds. The Willow Warbler appears a fortnight later.

Willow Warblers are extremely widespread in Britain and nest in almost any area of open woodland, scrub or overgrown hedge. Chiffchaffs like similar habitats (but only if there are tall trees available as song-posts) and they are usually less common in the north. Both species will nest in country gardens if they border a wood or have wild areas of scrub or thickets. They both build a domed nest rather like a Wren's but more open-fronted, and Willow Warblers usually build on the ground whereas Chiffchaffs nest off the ground but seldom higher than 1m (3ft).

Willow Warblers and most of the Chiffchaffs have left Britain by the beginning of October, but some of the latter remain until late autumn and a few even overwinter in the south of England.

Garden Warbler

A bird flitting about deep in a bramble patch that appears to have no distinctive features at all is probably a Garden Warbler (*Sylvia borin*). Seldom easy to see clearly, it is a uniform, rather plump, brownish warbler with paler underparts, a round head and stubby bill. Its presence is most obviously detected by its mellow warbling song which can easily be confused with the Blackcap's but is quieter and more sustained. However, all but the most experienced will need to catch a glimpse of the singer to be sure which is which.

In spite of its name, the Garden Warbler is not often found in gardens unless they are large with shrubberies or patches of brambles. It usually inhabits rather open broadleaved woodland with a thick shrub layer and will also nest in young plantations where the small trees still form a dense thicket. The male bird builds several 'cock nests' which are less substantial than the actual nest where the eggs are laid, which is built by both parents.

Although the main foods during the breeding season are insects and spiders, the Garden Warbler will also eat fruit such as raspberries, currants, cherries and blackberries.

The Garden Warbler's stay in Britain is short. Most birds arrive between late April and the end of May and leave again by mid-September.

Swift

A screaming group of Swifts (*Apus apus*) racing headlong over the roof-tops of our towns and villages must be one of the most haunting summer sounds. The most aerial of all our birds, the Swift is superbly adapted for life on the wing, catching its food, gathering nest material and even mating and sleeping without landing. It is easily distinguished from the House Martin and Swallow as it appears dark brown all over and its backward-pointing, sickle-shaped wings are much longer and thinner.

Observations from aircraft and on radar have shown that Swifts often fly to over 1 000 metres in height, and when food is abundant over high moorland they will travel many kilometres from their nest-sites. While foraging, the insects are stored in a throat pouch. The food gradually accumulates into a sticky lump mixed with saliva and the young are fed one food ball each.

Swifts breed under the eaves or in the cracks in old buildings. The recent demolition of many old houses and their replacement with modern buildings has severely reduced nest-sites. If you live in a modern house it is well worth making holes under the eaves to provide alternative accommodation; tunnel-like nest-boxes will prevent soiling of the roof space. However, you have to be patient for it may be several years before Swifts finally take up residence.

Not all modern developments have been detrimental, since the control of atmospheric pollution, for example, has allowed the Swift colonies in our city centres to increase.

Spotted Flycatcher

The Spotted Flycatcher (*Muscicapa striata*) is a drab, grey-brown bird the size of a sparrow, with a streaked crown and breast and paler underparts. Although it is no great songster, it always seems to win a special place in people's hearts when it nests in their garden.

Originally a bird of open woods or the forest edge, man-made habitats such as farmyards, gardens, parks and churchyards are ideal for it since they provide isolated trees, walls and posts from which the flycatcher can hunt for insects. It will sit bolt upright on one of these perches and suddenly make an erratic foray into the air to catch a passing insect with a loud snap of its bill.

Although it often nests among creepers on the side of a house, it seldom becomes at all tame. This adds to its fascination since one feels privileged that such a truly wild bird should have deigned to share one's garden, and people point out their flycatchers with pride.

The Spotted Flycatcher is one of our last migrants to arrive and does not normally appear in the garden before early May, by which time there are plenty of flying insects about. Each year I am just at the point of giving them up, when they return.

Spotted Flycatchers nest throughout mainland Britain only avoiding tree-less areas such as high mountains, open moors or fens. They are sparsely distri-buted in industrial Yorkshire, where pollution probably affects the flying insects on which they feed.

Collared Dove

Twenty years ago the very mention of a Collared Dove (*Streptopelia decaocto*) was enough to cause great excitement among birdwatchers. However, by 1977 they had been officially declared a pest species and were put on Schedule II of the Protection of Birds Acts.

The first pair bred in Norfolk in 1955 and by 1972 they were widespread through lowland Britain and much of Ireland, with an estimated population of 36–40 000 pairs. This dramatically successful colonization was possible because the Collared Dove found an ecological niche unfilled by any other species. Collared Doves live in close association with man and concentrate where grain is available – on quaysides, mills and places where livestock are fed. This constant supply of food has allowed them to breed throughout the year and thus increase at such a tremendous rate. Their nests are usually well hidden (unlike Woodpigeons) in evergreen trees such as cypress and pine or among ivy. This may also help to reduce predation and perhaps is another key to their success.

The Collared Dove can be distinguished from its close relative the Turtle Dove, which is a migrant, by its more uniform, creamy-buff plumage and pale primaries. Its monotonous, trisyllabic 'coo' contrasts with the soporific, purring song of the Turtle Dove.

Woodpigeon

Despite its name the Woodpigeon (*Columba palumbus*) is no longer solely a woodland bird. As areas were cleared for farming the Woodpigeon prospered and now has reached pest proportions causing damage worth hundreds of thousands of pounds a year. In gardens, it is a perfect pest destroying pea, bean and cabbage crops.

The Woodpigeon can be distinguished from the other grey doves which visit your garden – Stock Doves and the multicoloured Feral Pigeon – by its larger size, white wing flashes and the patches of white on the sides of its neck from which it gets the name Ring Dove.

During the breeding season the males utter their cooing song. They indicate their territory by a display, flying in an arc and clapping their wings; the sound being made by a whiplash effect and not by the wings hitting each other.

In urban areas where there is a plentiful supply of food, Woodpigeons breed from April until September. On farmland though, most birds do not lay until grain becomes readily available in July. Young pigeons or squabs, unlike most other young birds, are not dependent on a diet of insects for their necessary protein. Both the parents produce a special secretion from the wall of their crops known as 'pigeon's milk'. The secretion starts during the last days of incubation and is controlled by a hormone. It is therefore essential that there is an abundant food supply for the parents. The young leave the nest after about five weeks when the parents may be sitting on the next clutch. It is small wonder therefore, that the pigeon has always been a symbol of fertility.

Jackdaw

Jackdaws (*Corvus monedula*) are regular visitors to bird-tables in both the town and the country. They were recorded at a third of the places examined in the British Trust for Ornithology's survey of feeding stations. However, you will be lucky to see one on the bird-table for they steal in, grab a morsel and quickly rush off with it. They most often visit the garden first thing in the morning before anyone is about.

Jackdaws are jaunty birds with glossy black plumage and a smart grey nape and are perhaps the most appealing of the crow family. On a windy day they are a delight to watch as they perform spectacular aerobatics, twisting and tumbling as if for the sheer joy of it.

Usually, they nest in groups in holes in trees, buildings or cliffs but are not above completely blocking a chimney with a great mass of sticks. Paired birds remain together throughout the year and the colony is a strong social unit. All its members will attack a stranger or go to the aid of an individual in distress, driving off the attacker.

Jackdaws often associate with Rooks to feed on grassland where they eat beetles and other invertebrates. They also roost together; each evening a mixed flock flies over my house, the Jackdaws announcing themselves as they call 'jack, jack' to each other.

Moorhen

Moorhen (*Gallinula chloropus*) is a somewhat misleading name for this bird which is most common in the lowlands. Waterhen is far more apt as it is found wherever there is still or slow-flowing water. A tiny pond or a large, sluggish river are ideal provided they are surrounded by plenty of vegetation where the bird can seek shelter. Anyone whose garden borders a river or stream will be used to the sight of a Moorhen stalking across their lawn on outsized feet and flicking its tail to show the white flashes beneath. In a sheltered garden, Moorhens will become regular visitors pinching the scraps from beneath the bird-table.

If danger threatens, a Moorhen will rush for the nearest cover, or if it is swimming it will rapidly dive out of sight. The bird may even remain submerged for a considerable length of time by cunningly poking its bill above the surface of the water to draw in air.

Although seemingly rather amiable garden residents, Moorhens can be extremely aggressive to other birds and will kill young in nearby nests. Moorhens lay two or three clutches and the elder birds help their parents to rear the later broods. On the local village pond I have watched adult Moorhens hunt for food; each morsel was given to the elder chick which in turn fed its younger siblings in the nest.

Further reading

There is a bewildering number of bird books on the market. However, one of the first books anyone interested in birdwatching will need to buy is a field guide. The following are recommended:

Brunn, B and Singer, A *The Hamlyn Guide to Birds of Britain and Europe.* Hamlyn, London, 1970
Hayman, P and Burton P *The Birdlife of Britain.* Mitchell Beazley, London, 1976
Peterson, R T; Mountfort, G and Hollom, P A D *A Field Guide to the Birds of Britain and Europe.* Collins, London, 1966
Saunders, D *RSPB Guide to British Birds.* Hamlyn, London, 1975

The following books will help you to find out more about the habits of birds and how to study them:

Fisher, J and Flegg, J J M *Watching Birds.* Poyser, Berkhampstead, 1974
Fitter, R et al *Book of British Birds.* (Reader's Digest/ AA) Collins, 1969
Gooders, J *How to Watch Birds.* Andre Deutsch, London, 1975
Hollom, P A D *The Popular Handbook of British Birds.* Witherby, London, 1968
Lack, D *Life of the Robin.* Witherby, London, 1977
Murton, R *Man and Birds.* Collins, London, 1977
Newton, I *Finches.* Collins, London, 1972
Perrins, C *Birds.* Collins, London, 1974
Sharrock, T T R *The Atlas of Breeding Birds in Britain and Ireland.* (Irish Wildlife Conservancy) British Trust for Ornithology, Tring, 1976
Soper, T *Everday Birds.* David and Charles, Newton Abbott, 1976
Sparks, J *Bird Behaviour.* Hamlyn, London, 1969
——and Soper, T *Owls: their Natural and Unnatural History.* David and Charles, Newton Abbot, 1970

There are other books that deal with different aspects of birds and wildlife in the garden:

Barrington, R *The Bird Gardener's Book.* Wolfe, London, 1971
Burton, R *Ponds, their wildlife and upkeep.* David and Charles, Newton Abbot, 1977
Chinery, M *The Natural History of the Garden.* Collins, London, 1977
Flegg, J J M and Glue, D E *Nestboxes.* British Trust for Ornithology, Tring, 1971
Soper, T *The Bird Table Book in colour.* David and Charles, Newton Abbot, 1977
Soper, T *Wildlife begins at Home.* David and Charles, Newton Abbot, 1977

These books will be useful for those who want to improve their bird photography:

Hosking, E and Gooders, J *Wild Life Photography: a Field Guide.* Hutchinson, London, 1973
Marchington, J and Clay, A *An Introduction to Bird and Wildlife Photography.* Faber and Faber, London, 1974

Bird conservation societies

The Royal Society for the Protection of Birds, The Lodge, Sandy, Bedfordshire.

This organization owns or leases 74 reserves covering more than 80,000 acres in Britain and Northern Ireland and plays a vital part in conserving wild birds and the places where they live. Equally important is its work in the enforcement of the bird protection laws, conservation planning, research and education including film production and publishing. However, perhaps most important of all, the RSPB is the country's strongest conservation lobby with over a quarter of a million members. The full colour, illustrated magazine *Birds* is sent free of charge to members every quarter.

The Young Ornithologists' Club, The Lodge, Sandy, Bedfordshire.

This is the junior section of the RSPB for young people 15 years of age and under. The club organizes projects, outings and courses, and members receive their own bimonthly magazine *Bird Life*.

The British Trust for Ornithology, Beech Grove, Tring, Hertfordshire.

This is recommended for birdwatchers who enjoy ornithological field work since its members join in active field studies, ringing and census work. The BTO always has a number of projects on the go both organized from headquarters and run by individuals. Members are kept informed by a six-weekly newsletter, *BTO News*, and a quarterly journal, *Bird Study*.

The Society for the Promotion of Nature Conservation, The Green, Nettleham, Lincolnshire.

This is an organization that coordinates the work of the Country Trusts for Nature Conservation. All areas, either a single county or groups of counties, have their own individual Trust. The Trusts acquire and manage reserves for all forms of wildlife, which are usually of local rather than national interest. They are actively involved in the effects of county planning decisions on wildlife.

Index